CLEMATIS

■ For Colour and Versatility ■

Keith & Carol Fair

CROWOOD GARDENING GUIDES

First published in 1990 by
The Crowood Press Ltd
Ramsbury, Marlborough
Wiltshire SN8 2HR

This impression 1995

British Library Cataloguing in Publication Data

Fair, Keith
  Clematis.
  I. Gardens. Clematis
  I. Title II. Fair, Carol
  635.9'33111
ISBN 1 85223 284 6

Picture Credits
All photographs by the authors, except Figs 4, 46 and 51 by Jan Fopma, Figs 33,
36, 56 and 60 by Linda Burgess, and Figs 40, 53, 59 and 65 by Naoki Uehara.

The photograph on the title page shows 'Horn of Plenty'; on page 4 are two
summer-flowering viticellas in the author's garden: (left) 'Madame Julia
Correvon', and (right) 'Etoile Violette', on the front cover is 'Ruby Glow', and on
the back cover (top) 'Henryi', and (bottom) 'Haku Ookan'.

All line-drawings by Claire Upsdale-Jones.

Typeset by Chippendale Type, Otley, West Yorkshire.
Printed and bound by the Paramount Printing Group, Hong Kong.

Contents

Acknowledgements

Although we work with clematis daily, and are familiar with all the aspects of their growing that are discussed within this book, we are grateful for the advice and assistance we have received from friends both within and outside the horticultural industry, who have helped our research and checked some of the information given herein. In particular, we would like to express our thanks to Mr Jan Fopma of Boskoop in Holland who, in addition to being a knowledgeable ear on the end of the phone to whom we could refer points of doubt, spent many hours reading the initial draft of the book, and drew our attention to inaccuracies, omissions and some ambiguities. We are also indebted to Dr Jim Johnston of Lincoln for checking some of the historical detail and finding other references from which we could work.

Preface

Most clematis seen in gardens are bought without much thought, receive the minimum of care and give great delight to their owners. This book is written for those who have had problems or want a reference book which will help them if things do not grow quite as planned. Basically, growing clematis is enjoyable, rewarding and mostly a matter of common sense. If you look through a medical reference book, you may end up thinking you will be lucky to last out the night! Similarly, if you consider all the pitfalls which you can encounter growing clematis, none would be sold. However, if a book is to help, it has to try to cover most aspects of their growth, although the authors know only too well that, in practice, any one person may need only a fraction of the advice offered.

Fig 1 This is perhaps everybody's idea of what a clematis should look like – 'Nelly Moser'.

Introduction

The country cottage garden, bursting with the flowers of roses, honeysuckle, hollyhocks and lupins, with a clematis growing over the front porch, is perhaps the image at the back of the mind of many, as they cultivate the small patch which is their garden in these days of over-priced land and ever denser housing. Despite neglect, the roses will bloom, the honeysuckle will attempt to show some colour, ignoring the attentions of a myriad of aphids, and the hollyhocks will flower through a haze of rust; even the lupins will defy the sometimes harsh ravages of an English summer and make an attempt to flower.

For many, however, it is the clematis climbing over the front porch which is the most reward-ing. Every year it brings a great splash of colour to the house, and raises the spirits of its owners with its display, which can always be relied upon once it has been established. It is this reliability that has attracted gardeners to it for many generations. In 1935, just before he died at the age of 96, William Robinson of Gravetye Manor in Sussex wrote of clematis: 'They are as hardy as the British oak, come early into flower and only cease with the approach of winter. I believe them to be the finest of all hardy flowers.' Their popularity has remained to this day, and the vast majority of gardens exhibit at least one specimen. Indeed, we know of a number throughout the country that house collections of a hundred or more. Many of these gardens are quite small but their owners still find room for 'just one more' – clematis can be used in so many ways, from massive screening operations masking eyesores, to neat patio plants in tubs.

THE FLOWERING SEASON

As a genus, or family of plants, clematis have an extremely long flowering season. As they bloom in the garden, it would seem that each period of a few weeks brings forth a different shape of clematis, for the size, form and, to some extent, the colour of the flowers are related to the time of year. The first 'hardy as British oak' types of clematis to come into bloom are the alpinas and macropetalas, which emerge out of a froth of bright green, finely-cut leaves as early as April. Blue is the natural colour of both these varieties, but there are also many good cultivars ranging from white and pink through to mauve.

Following hard on their heels in late May and June are the montanas, whose simple pink or white star-like flowers create an impenetrable mass of bloom, often yielding a sweet scent reminiscent of chocolate or vanilla as the sun catches the blooms on a warm evening. In early June, the pink and white striped cartwheels of 'Nelly Moser' delight with their size and uniform-ity as they frame many a cottage door. 'Nelly Moser' is typical of the range of two-tone pink and white or pink and mauve clematis to be found at this time of year. A wonderful range of lavender blues, deep pinks, mauves and whites are to be found in the single colour varieties, as well as (but only occasionally), rich violet and purple.

The size of the flowers increases in early summer. There are the fully double blooms of varieties like 'Vyvyan Pennell', or the huge simple blooms produced by hybrids such as 'W. E. Gladstone'. If they are happy in their

Fig 2 Clematis macropetala *'Rosy O'Grady' – early-flowering and very hardy.*

Fig 3 Clematis montana *growing over a town gate.*

situation, these can cover a whole area of wall with spectacular flowers of about 10in (25cm) in diameter. As summer progresses, the flower size diminishes, the spectacular individual flowers of the mid-season hybrids being replaced by the splendour of the massed blooms of the hard-pruning cultivars. There is a dramatic change in colour, the pale blues and whites become scarce, but there are numerous wine-reds, purples and violets from which to choose. The small-flowered *viticella* varieties, that have been described as the 'montanas of summer', appear amongst the foliage of trees and shrubs from July onwards.

In late summer and autumn, berries and fruits begin to show, with the species clematis displaying their produce in the form of silky, tassel-like seed heads, which almost surpass the

flowers in their beauty. It is within the range of species varieties that the only true yellow clematis are to be found. Summer ends with a froth of yellow and white small flowers, many of which are scented. In July and August, the herbaceous clematis with their bell-shaped or hyacinth-like flowers also come into their own; they too are often fragrant. Flowers that frequently give the most pleasure are the occasional blooms late in the year of the hybrid cultivars growing in a sheltered spot. In a favourable year these will often hang on until the New Year, although these late blooms tend to be a little the worse for the ravages of earwigs, gales and sub-zero temperatures.

Fig 4 *The double* viticella *type,* C. viticella *'Purpurea Plena Elegans'.*

THE CHOICE

The variations in flower type are also matched by differences in vigour and habit. Some clematis make neat compact plants whilst others billow forth in a riotous manner. Several specialist nurseries offer for sale between one hundred and fifty and two hundred varieties, and there are many more in cultivation, so the question of choice can present immense difficulties for the serious purchaser. You must do some homework. The practical considerations, such as suitability for the chosen site, height of the plant and its flowering time, can be researched – much of the basic information is in the catalogues or the tables in this book. However, it is the appearance of the actual flower which remains elusive; words and two-dimensional photographs can never match up to the reality of a three-dimensional flower, whose colours will change in different lights and whose sepals can vary in surface from smooth and glossy, to ribbed, or even richly velvety. The gardener with some experience of clematis will be able to formulate an impression of the flower shape when he reads the description, which will refer to 'overlapping sepals' or 'crenulated edges', but the actual colour will almost certainly be elusive. The colour of each flower changes so much, from the newly-opened bloom to the time of sepal fall, and with some varieties there is a marked difference between early and late flowers, both in colour and size. The colour and size of flowers can also vary from one year to the next, depending on the warmth of the season.

For anyone who is new to clematis, the choice can be bewildering. People sometimes choose to buy a clematis specifically for its ability to cover buildings and areas of the garden which they consider eyesores – clematis and, perhaps, climbing roses planted along the length of an old brick wall can turn it into a delight. Most clematis, however, are bought primarily for their flowers. Many customers will turn to the nurseryman or sales assistant for advice on their purchase, and the majority will be only too willing, but they will need to be given help as well. It is easy to provide a variety that should flourish in a given situation, but will the customer actually like the flower? Does he want small or large blooms, and what about the colour? 'I don't want one of your pyjama stripes,' was a very useful comment made by a purchaser of one of the early-flowering hybrids – many were immediately eliminated!

Photographs and Descriptions

The representation of colour in gardening literature can be misleading, and should only be

9

used as a guide in conjunction with a written description. The words used in some of the descriptions of colour can also be confusing, particularly 'blue' and 'red'. The interpretation of a colour from a word is a subjective process, and a 'good blue' will mean different things to different readers. If they conjure up an image of the blue associated with gentians or delphiniums, they will be disappointed to find that it does not exist in clematis. The blues of clematis always have some trace of mauve, so they tend towards lavender rather than 'true blue'. Similarly, the reds, with the exception of C. texensis 'Gravetye Beauty', all have a certain degree of blue in their composition, making them magenta, wine-red or maroon rather than scarlet. There is a wonderfully subtle range of colour within the genus, but disappointment can occur when a faded picture label, whose original magenta has lost its red and turned blue, is taken at its face value and doesn't match up to the final flower.

Size of flower is another problem when choosing from an illustration. The major growers' catalogues all give an indication of the diameter of the flower, but there is usually nothing in a photograph or picture label to give it a sense of scale. For example, a close-up of a white montana whose flower might measure 2in (5cm) in diameter, could look very similar to a distant shot of 'Marie Boisselot' with a diameter of 8in (20cm). Not only is the size of the bloom a consideration, but the character of flowers can vary. 'Mrs Cholmondeley' or 'Beauty of Richmond', are both very large, rather floppy and lavender blue, and their gappy sepals would delight many people with

their sheer size and exuberance, except, of course, the person who likes a neat, well-rounded flower with overlapping sepals – 'H. F. Young' or 'Alice Fisk' would be much more to their taste.

The problem of misinterpretation applies particularly to some of the species clematis. Many of them achieve their magnificence by a great mass of flower burgeoning forth from a mature specimen, and the individual flowers are something of a nonentity. Once again, the limited description in a catalogue can be misleading without a general understanding of the genus. We have had an incensed customer complain that the two C. jouiniana 'Præcox' flowers that had just opened on his plant looked more like 'dead nettles' than 'hyacinth-like' as described in the catalogue! This was a case of the standard description of the plant being taken too literally. Certainly, those two flowers would look insignificant by themselves, since they don't have the individual charm of, say, the flower of an alpina. However, en masse, as ground cover, they are admirable.

This book sets out to help the beginner overcome these problems and achieve a display that he has only seen in the gardens of others. It is also intended to help the successful to extend their knowledge in order that they may begin to realise the full potential of the species, no matter how inhospitable their garden. Whilst some may wish to read from cover to cover, the book is written so that it may be used for reference, and it can be dipped into at any point for specific information without the need to read the whole.

Fig 5 Clematis orientalis 'Bill Mackenzie'.

CHAPTER 1

Background and History

To the non-botanist, the plant family into which a particular genus is grouped is often surprising. The genus *Clematis* is no exception, as it belongs to the family *Ranunculaceae,* which also includes hellebores, delphiniums, peonies, anemones, buttercups and king cups. So what are the connections between the tall, climbing clematis with its hard spindly stem, and the usually low-growing, fleshy plants within the same family? The most obvious similarity is that they all benefit from growing in a rich moist soil. Also, study of the flowers will show a notable visual affinity between branches of the family – the rounded, slightly cupped hellebores or king cups could be likened to some of the montanas, whilst single and double anemones bear a resemblance to the large-flowered clematis varieties. Another, less immediately obvious, similarity between them is that clematis and some other flowers within the family such as *Caltha* (king cup), do not have petals as such – it is the sepals that form the colourful part of the flower. Clematis are exceptional in their family in that a majority are woody climbers, although there is a much smaller group of non-climbing herbaceous varieties together with some woody sub-shrubs.

There are some hundreds of clematis species distributed throughout the world, primarily in the cool-temperate northern hemisphere, but many of these are of little horticultural interest. The large-flowered hybrid as we know it today is a comparatively modern flower dating from the middle of the nineteenth century. Possibly the earliest references to clematis in Britain were made in the sixteenth-century herbals. The native *C. vitalba* was referred to as 'Hedge

Vine' by William Turner in his *The Names of Herbs* (1548), and as 'Travellers Joy' by John Gerard in the *Herball* of 1597.

Clematis have been grown in English gardens since *C. viticella* was brought over from Spain in 1569. This tiny, purple, bell-shaped flower was given the name 'Virgin's Bower' in honour of Queen Elizabeth I. During her reign an interest

Fig 6 Two Jackmanii *clematis framing the door of a Lincolnshire cottage.*

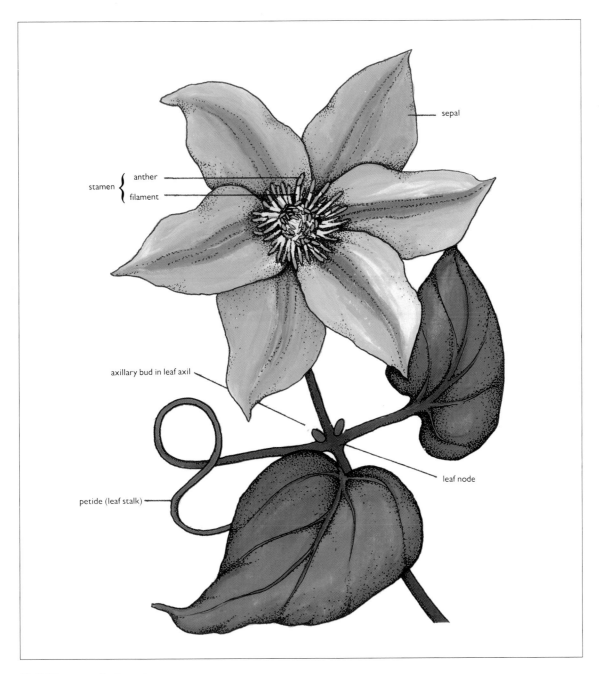

Fig 7 The parts of a clematis.

Fig 8 Named after his wife, clematis 'Mrs George Jackman' is perhaps one of George Jackman's most successful varieties.

in botany and plants developed, and as travel became more possible a number of species from the Continent were introduced: *C. integrifolia* from Hungary, *C. cirrhosa* from the Balearic Islands and *C. recta* from southern Europe. During the seventeenth and eighteenth centuries, *C. flammula*, *C. orientalis* and *C. alpina* were also introduced; these are, of course, all small-flowered varieties which are still grown in this country today.

During the mid-nineteenth century and the early part of the twentieth, there was a tremendous frenzy of plant hunting and new species of all types were introduced into Western Europe. Three large-flowered clematis from China and Japan – namely *C. florida*, *C. patens* and *C. lanuginosa* – stimulated an interest in hybridisation. Both *C. florida* and *C. patens* have made a significant contribution to the large-flowered hybrid as we now know it, but it was the very large pale blue *C. lanuginosa* that was responsible for the size that is to be found in such varieties as 'W. E. Gladstone'. An interest

in hybridisation developed, one of the first successes being *C. x jackmanii*, created by George Jackman of Woking in 1858. He took *C. lanuginosa* and crossed it with *C. eriostemon* and *C. viticella*. The result was the deep purple flower that has remained one of the most popular varieties to this day. When this plant was exhibited five years later, it caused a sensation, and clematis breeding on a large scale burst forth in Britain, France, Germany and Belgium. This enthusiasm was sustained for about thirty years, and in that time hundreds of new cultivars were introduced and given glowing recommendations. Some of these have stood the test of time and are still with us, but many others have vanished.

A number of plants were, of course, named after the nurserymen themselves and their families; for example, 'Jackmanii', 'Mrs George Jackman,' 'Barbara Jackman', and 'Belle of Woking' all came from the famous Surrey firm of Messrs Jackman of Woking. This practice of naming clematis after family and employees in

Fig 9 'Richard Pennell', named by Walter Pennell after his son.

Fig 10 An herbaceous clematis, C. heracleifolia *'Wyevale', growing in a mixed border.*

the nursery has continued; the late Walter Pennell of Lincoln introduced varieties like 'C. W. Dowman', 'Herbert Johnson', 'H. F. Young', 'Jim Hollis', 'Ken Donson', as well as those he named after his own family. He made perhaps the greatest single contribution to serious hybridisation in this country since the great pioneers of the late nineteenth century. Working between 1950 and 1962, he raised 26 new varieties, many of them acclaimed world-wide. 'Vyvyan Pennell', named after his wife, is the most well known of these.

Another name synonymous with clematis in this country is that of Jim Fisk of Westleton in Suffolk. Not only has he produced some new hybrids of his own, but he has also been instrumental in introducing into the market a number of new varieties raised by his customers. He has also forged links with other countries, thus providing the British customer with many excellent varieties from Poland, Japan and Argentina.

We seem at the moment to be experiencing a renaissance in clematis hybridisation. The activity is perhaps less frenetic than it was at the end of the last century, but it is certainly an international enthusiasm. In recent years, a number of other growers in the UK have introduced some noteworthy varieties and many more are at the trial stage. Wonderful hardy varieties, both *alpina* and *macropetala* cultivars and large-flowered hybrids, are currently being raised in Sweden. Good macropetalas have been introduced to Europe from Canada, whilst new varieties from Russia are currently being assessed by different growers in Western Europe. Additionally, plant hunters are still bringing back hitherto unknown species of clematis from the wild. Much is going on, and many new varieties are being popularised, although inevitably in another hundred years many of them will be lost to cultivation. A few will have stood the test of time, together with those of the early hybridisers, which will by then be over two hundred years old!

CHAPTER 2

Cultivation

CLEMATIS IN THE WILD

'Weeds seem to be the only things that will grow well in my garden,' you will hear people say, in a frustrated moment, after a walk around their garden when all did not look quite as they had hoped. By 'weeds' they mean wild flowers. However, a closer look will show that only some 'weeds' will survive in their patch. Because of the particular conditions which exist in their area, other weeds simply will not grow. In theory, many clematis could be classed as weeds, for they are the wild plants of other countries. Visitors to some parts of northern Provence in France will not have to look far to see new house owners clearing and burning tangles of *Clematis flammula* from what will become their garden. The only wild clematis native to the British Isles is *C. vitalba*, more commonly known as 'Old Man's Beard' or 'Traveller's Joy', which grows in profusion in some parts of the country. It is by studying the conditions in which *C. vitalba* thrives that we can begin to understand the basic requirements for many of its cultivated cousins.

'*Vitalba* is a hedgerow plant' – from these five words what can we find out about its requirements? What can we learn from its love of the hedgerows of the Cotswolds, and its seeming dislike of the Essex marshes? Firstly, consider the hedgerow. Many hedgerows have been in existence far longer than is often realised – old Ordnance Survey maps will show a majority of the hedges we know today in place a hundred years ago, and most can be traced on the documents relating to the Enclosure Acts between 1780 and 1830. Many

can even be found on the 'Tithe Award' maps, which go back much further, and a few have their origins in Saxon times, being well over a thousand years old. Out of interest, the date of a hedge can be roughly determined by multiplying the number of species of tree and shrub in a

Fig 11 The seed heads of C. vitalba *(Old Man's Beard) can brighten the garden in midwinter.*

30-metre length by 100. Thus, if a 30-metre length contains six species, the hedge is probably about 600 years old. (Prof. W. G. Hoskins and Dr Max Hooper.) It is possible that the hedgerows alongside the Fosse Way in the Midlands, which can be seen festooned with *C. vitalba* seed heads in the late autumn, might have been there in one form or another since the Romans first constructed the road, through what was probably mixed woodland. It is not unreasonable to suppose that 'Old Man's Beard' has been growing happily along this stretch of road for nearly two thousand years.

What does this type of hedge have to offer the wild clematis? Why is it such a good host? Initially it provides the nutrient. In autumn and winter, much dead vegetation is blown into the hedge bottom by the gales, where it collects, rots and eventually forms a fine, rich leaf mould. As this accumulates over the decades and centuries, the soil level on which the hedge grows is very gradually raised. This raised area

of soil drains quickly after the rain, a process which is accelerated if the hedge has been planted on a bank with a ditch beside it. The leaf mould helps retain sufficient moisture to sustain the shallow-rooted plants during drier periods. The hedge itself also breaks the wind and shades the soil at its roots from the sun, again slowing down the natural drying that occurs in more open situations. From these factors, we may conclude that clematis like a moist, but well-drained soil. However, they do not like the soil to be too wet. *Vitalba* seeds falling on damp marshland may germinate and grow well for a while, but their roots will rot away in the winter when the land becomes waterlogged. The leaf mould not only retains a good balance of moisture, but it also is a source of rich nutrient. From this we should quickly realise that clematis are gross feeders.

Many newcomers will have been told to cover the root area of clematis with stone slabs. These slabs do the same job as the hedge in

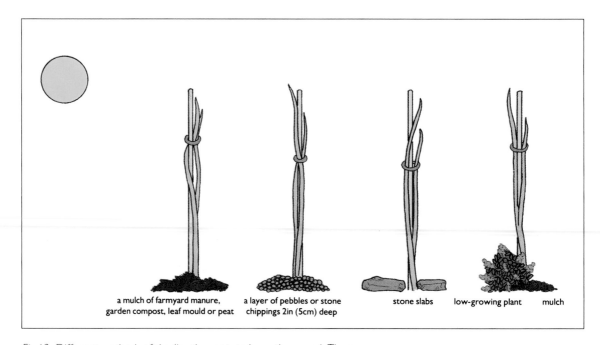

a mulch of farmyard manure, garden compost, leaf mould or peat | a layer of pebbles or stone chippings 2in (5cm) deep | stone slabs | low-growing plant | mulch

Fig 12 Different methods of shading the roots to keep them cool. The area covered should be about 20in (50cm) in diameter.

keeping the ground cool and helping to retain moisture. Clematis seem to grow quite well if their roots are not cool; it is the dampness that is important. Low-growing bushes and shrubs will be just as effective as the slabs in keeping the ground cool. However, the gardener must make sure that there is enough moisture to meet the needs of both the clematis and shrub.

SOIL

The native clematis, *vitalba*, grows wild in chalk or limestone country, and this seems to have given rise to the misconception that garden cultivars need an alkaline soil. Certainly they are very happy in such an area, but they will grow perfectly well in neutral or quite acid conditions, although where there is a low pH many gardeners include mortar when planting, and lime annually. Much more important than the acidity or alkalinity is the *type* of soil. Thinking back to the hedgerow, the ideal soil for clematis is a rich, well-drained, friable loam. However, many people have to garden on light sandy soils or heavy wet clay.

On sandy soils clematis will grow, but usually only with diminished vigour. The main problem is a lack of moisture which, in turn, leads to a loss of nutrients. The large particles of sand mean that these soils are very free-draining, which makes them not only dry but hungry, as any fertilisers applied are quickly washed away. There is also a tendency for such soils to heat up quickly in a dry spell. Preparation of the planting site must be extra thorough; surface mulching with organic matter is essential, and even then it will be a constant battle to provide sufficient water and nutrient to grow good clematis. Thin soils over chalk can present similar difficulties.

Clay soils are less of a problem, provided they are not actually waterlogged. In areas where the water table rises badly in winter, tile drainage would be necessary. If the ground is not subject to actual flooding, but the sides of

the planting hole are pure clay when dug out and it quickly fills up with water, steps have to be taken to open up the subsoil. To achieve this, the first spit of reasonable topsoil should be dug out and put to one side. The next spit, of what will probably be sticky clay in winter and something like concrete in the summer, should be removed and discarded. The topsoil which was initially put to one side can now be mixed with an equal quantity by volume of sharp grit, and placed in the hole at subsoil level. Humus or other organic matter can now be forked in and the hole filled with good garden soil or John Innes No. 3. The addition of grit to the subsoil opens up the structure of the clay to increase the drainage. The inclusion of organic material is of specific importance as it not only soaks up excess moisture, but also alters the structure of the clay soil by creating larger particles, thus improving aeration and drainage. Clematis are moisture-loving plants, and they only do well in clay soil if the amount of moisture is not too great, and the soil structure is sufficiently open to prevent compaction around the roots.

With regard to the correct type of humus to incorporate in the soil, any well-decayed vegetable matter will do, including leaf mould, mushroom compost, farmyard manure, peat, ground bark, and so on. It all depends what is available in the locality at low cost. However, as peat and ground bark have no real food value, and act purely as soil conditioners, they should only be used in conjunction with a good general fertiliser.

PLANTING

When to Plant

Clematis sold today are container grown and can be planted at any time of the year without root disturbance, but clearly it would be unwise to plant during a summer drought or when the ground is frozen or waterlogged. Clematis

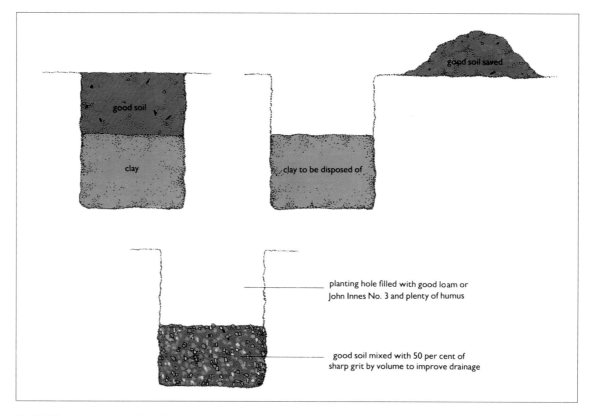

good soil saved

good soil

clay

clay to be disposed of

planting hole filled with good loam or
John Innes No. 3 and plenty of humus

good soil mixed with 50 per cent of
sharp grit by volume to improve drainage

Fig 13 The preparation of the planting hole on a heavy clay soil.

planted in midsummer do need careful water-ing, and the success or failure of those put in at this time seems to be determined by whether the new owner is on hand to water or not. The gardener who plants, however carefully, and then goes on holiday for two or three weeks is likely to return to a dead clematis if there has been a dry spell in his absence.

Some people have very definite preferences for either autumn or spring planting. On a light soil, autumn planting is favoured, so that the plant can get established before the dry weather which so often occurs in the spring. People who garden on very heavy clay find they incur more losses as a result of autumn planting, owing to the waterlogging of inadequately drained soil. They, therefore, have a preference for the drier conditions of the spring. On well-drained loam,

planting can safely take place any time between September and the end of March, when the weather is mild and the ground workable.

A majority of clematis in normal cultivation are perfectly hardy and able to withstand the normal British winter, even before they become fully established, but the evergreen varieties are better planted in the spring.

How to Plant

Much of the ultimate success of a clematis can be put down to the care with which it was chosen for its site, and the way in which it was planted. After a few years of growing in ideal conditions and being tended with loving care, most varieties will be so well established that they will withstand all but the most determined efforts to kill them.

When clematis are offered for sale they will generally have spent one and a half to two years in a nursery where, hopefully, they will have been looked after in ideal conditions, so that when they are planted in the garden, they will give many years of enjoyment. A nurseryman can only advise and hope that his advice is followed, but if the plants he sells are not then transferred to the right conditions, they will not thrive.

More clematis are probably lost through bad planning and planting than as a result of any other single factor. Many would-be gardeners look at the pot, think it isn't a very large plant, dig a small hole with a trowel, tread in the clematis, and finish the whole job in five minutes. Some are lucky, when conditions happen to be just right and the plant does well. Far more plants die or disappoint because the conditions are wrong, reflecting the lack of care taken in the initial planting. The nurseryman has probably put in eighteen months or more hard work and care, so it is worth taking at least half an hour or so to plan where the clematis should be and to plant it properly in its final position in the garden.

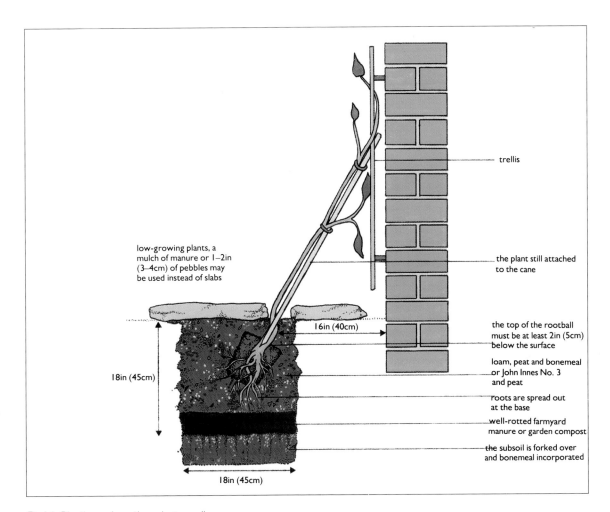

Fig 14 Planting a clematis against a wall.

When choosing a site for your plant, remember it needs a damp, well-drained spot, preferably with some protection from the wind. Avoid areas which you know dry out badly in the summer, or which are always exposed to the worst of the winds. Additionally, remember that clematis will not survive in situations where they can become waterlogged for weeks on end in the winter. Walls and large trees also absorb moisture from the soil, so it is helpful to minimise this competition for the available supply by planting the clematis 20–40in (50–100cm) out from a wall and subsequently training the plant back when it has made sufficient growth. If you are planning to run your clematis into a tree, choose a position outside the umbrella of the tree, where it will get plenty of light and moisture, and then train it into the tree only when it is large enough. (*See* Chapter 6.)

For the plant grown in the usual 4½–5in (11–12cm) pot, it is necessary to dig a hole about 18in (45cm) square and deep. The depth is important, but if a square is impossible because of obstructions, any shape of similar volume will suffice. If the space available does not allow for such a large hole, then you should ask yourself whether the site is really suitable. Some plants are sold in larger pots, either because it is the nurseryman's preference or because the plant is much older. In such cases, especially if the plant has made a great deal of root growth and looks nearly pot-bound, a larger, deeper hole would be necessary. If there is no great quantity of root the normal 18in (45cm) hole will probably be sufficient. Fork two or three handfuls of bonemeal into the bottom of the hole, and then, if you have it, fill the next 6in (15cm) with well-rotted farmyard manure. Fork this well into the bottom of the hole.

Before putting your new plant in the soil,

Fig 15 'Bee's Jubilee'.

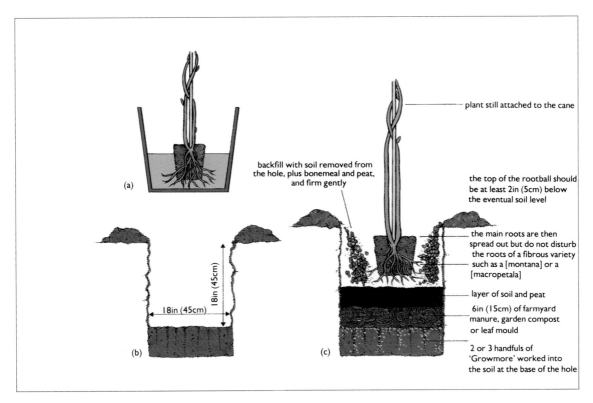

Fig 16 Planting. (a) If the clematis is at all dry, soak it in water for 10–20 minutes. (b) Dig a hole 18in (45cm) square and deep, and fork the soil at the bottom and sides to loosen it. (c) Prepare the nutrients to provide nourishment for the plant once it is established. (d) If the surrounding soil is dry, the plant should be watered in.

examine it carefully. If it has dried out at all, soak it for a while in a bucket of water. Cut off the bottom few leaves with a sharp knife or pair of scissors, and aim to plant your clematis at a depth which will cover the next set of buds up the stem. This is particularly important with large-flowered varieties – by planting to this depth you are burying some spare buds, which will start to grow if the upper part of the plant is damaged in any way. It is, if you like, an insurance policy which will help your plant survive if it is cut back by the weather, pests, or even inadvertently by someone who loses control of his hoe! Deep planting of clematis also stimulates stem rooting, a process to be encouraged in young plants.

When you take the plant out of its pot, look at the root system. If your plant is one of the species or small-flowered varieties, there is a good chance it will have a fibrous root system. If this is the case, disturb these roots as little as possible in planting. However, all the large-flowered varieties, and some species clematis have spaghetti-like roots, rather like couch grass, which can often grow round and round the base of the pot and will hang like a large spring when removed from it. Such roots should be carefully teased out and spread as the clematis is planted. Add some more peat and bonemeal to the soil as the hole is filled, firming the soil by treading gently. Should the soil in your garden be particularly poor, the hole could be filled with John Innes Compost

No. 3 to which more peat has been added. The peat is particularly important at this point because, in common with most plants bought from nurseries these days, your clematis will probably have been growing in a peat-based compost in its pot. Research has shown that, if there is no link between the growing medium used in the nursery and the soil in the garden, many types of plants have difficulty in making the transition between growing in peat and growing in soil. This has resulted in cases of plants which, some years after planting, have made no root growth at all beyond the small ball of peat in which they were first grown. Apart from helping to retain moisture in dry spells, peat introduced into the surrounding soil does help the plant to make this transition.

It is worth noting that clematis which are planted in the late autumn or early spring will very often show new growth near the base. These new shoots are most important, as they will become the main stems for the next season's growth. They are very brittle and will need to be handled with great care if they are not to be damaged.

There are also many thousands of smaller plants, packed in a polythene bag with a picture of their flower, sold by chainstores, super-markets and some garden centres in the spring. When sold, most of these clematis are less than a year old and are little more than rooted cuttings. Although, ultimately, they will give just as good a result as the larger plant, they do need a much greater degree of care if they are to succeed. When they are unpacked their roots are sometimes dry and should be soaked in water for about half an hour before you proceed further. Because of the packing and the conditions in which they have been kept, the stem will probably have become drawn and be pale in colour. With a sharp knife, cut this back to a good pair of buds about 3in (7.5cm) above the roots. Try to leave a further set below these. If you have a cold frame or unheated glasshouse, put your plant into a 4½in (11cm) pot using a reliable peat-based compost.

Keep damp, but not over-watered, and stand the pot on a bed of gravel. When your clematis has reached a height of 20in (50cm), plant in exactly the same way as already detailed for larger plants.

If you do not have a glasshouse or cold frame, prepare a site as before, but fill the hole with a peat-based compost mixed with 50 per cent soil. Plant the small clematis in this, first cutting off the bottom leaves and burying it so that one pair of buds are just below the surface. Cut off the growing stem at about 40–60in (100–150cm) above the surface. Use water to firm the plant instead of treading it in and cover with a small propagator top. This cover protects the plant from both the extremes of weather and from the unwanted attentions of slugs, who seem to regard clematis as a real delicacy. Remove this cover as soon as the plant really starts to grow, and tie the shoots to a small bamboo cane. Twigs positioned around it would give some protection from the wind. By the late summer, you should have a good plant which may, depending on the variety, reward you with some flowers late in the year.

Planting Distances

As a general rule, the large-flowered hybrids can be planted about 60–80in (150–200cm) apart, to give reasonable coverage on a wall or fence. Two varieties can be planted together so that their flowers may intermingle, but it is wise to choose two of the same pruning type, otherwise difficulties can arise! Varieties can be chosen to provide a pleasing colour association, or a shorter plant can be usefully employed to mask the non-flowering stem on a tall-growing cultivar.

AFTER CARE

There are many excellent clematis throughout the length and breadth of the country that are never watered and never fed, often thrusting

Fig 17 Clematis can grow quite happily together. Here 'Proteus' is growing alongside an unpruned 'Niobe'.

themselves skywards from the most unlikely little holes in the ground, or planted hard against the house wall, contravening all the advice given in books and magazines. When a clematis happily flourishes in an improbable situation, it is evident that there must be, in the subterranean depths, reserves of food and water on which it is able to draw: large blooms of good colour and healthy foliage are the result of a good diet. Clematis are gross feeders, and the large-flowered hybrids in particular will soon demonstrate that they are underfed.

Watering

In times of normal rainfall, established plants, well planted in a good moisture-retentive soil, should not require a great deal of watering. However, in a drought, they would certainly welcome a good soaking twice a week. Young plants in their first year with no depth of root, and those in their second year, in positions where they might be competing for moisture with neighbouring plants and buildings, should certainly not be allowed to dry out at any time. Established plants, in containers growing against south-facing walls or planted in very light sandy soils, will need constant watering in dry weather. A large plant in full leaf can use 1 gallon (4·5 litres) or more of water a day in hot weather. A really good soaking every two or three days is preferable to a splash a day. A hard-baked soil can be extremely difficult to penetrate, as the water from a can, even one fitted with a fine rose, tends to run off the surface. A winter mulch can help to act as a reservoir, or use the old tomato grower's trick of sinking a plant pot or length of pipe beside the clematis when it is planted. Water poured into the container is not then wasted, as it is delivered directly to the roots. It is quite an effective method, but waiting for the water to drain out of the bottom can sometimes be time-consuming! The top of the container needs to be kept covered or it will quickly fill up with debris, and become a refuge for slugs and earwigs.

Old plants often reveal a deep-seated drought and lack of nutrient by producing smaller and smaller flowers each year. Clematis eventually produce an extensive root system and the surrounding soil can dry out. This problem can usually be rectified by sinking a pipe into the ground, some distance from the main stem, to a depth of about 20in (50cm). The plant can then be given several cans of water via the pipe in the spring, and every so often subsequently during the growing season. It is beneficial to combine this with a programme of liquid feeding.

Feeding

If it is available, a mulch of well-rotted farmyard manure is the best autumn feed for clematis. It can be applied quite thickly, but must not be allowed to touch the stems, as it may cause damage. An area of about 5in (12cm) around the stem should be left clear. If such manure is not easily obtainable, two or three handfuls of bonemeal or general fertiliser can be gently forked into the surrounding soil, away from the main stem and taking care not to damage any new shoots which might be just under the surface. A mulch of peat, or ground and composted bark, may then be applied to help conserve moisture. In the spring, a handful of sulphate of potash sprinkled round each plant, and then watered in, will be beneficial for the flower development and colour. It also helps to prevent some varieties such as 'Mrs Cholmondeley' and 'Dawn' turning green early in the year.

If the autumn feeding has been inadequate or if the plants are growing in tubs or hungry soils, a weekly feed of tomato fertiliser would be profitable. This must never be applied to plants that are dry, as it may damage their fine roots; they should always be watered first. Clematis can be liquid-fed during the growing season, from early April to mid-August, but not when they are in bloom, as an excess of nutrient at this time tends to shorten the flowering period. Adequate watering, coupled with liquid feeding, is particularly necessary to boost the early-summer-flowering hybrids for their second flush of bloom in August and September.

MOVING AN ESTABLISHED PLANT

People do occasionally manage to move a clematis at the height of summer, but the only time when success can reasonably be expected is when the plant is dormant or just starting into growth in early spring. The older the plant, the more difficult the job, and the smaller the chance of success.

The top growth must be removed to just above a pair of strong leaf axil buds, but do not cut into an old stem that shows no sign of life low down. Such stems need to be cut further up where new growth has recently been made, again cutting above two suitable buds. Where possible, the plant should be cut back to about 20in (50cm), and the remaining stems should be tied to a bamboo cane to provide support and minimise damage to the stem wood. Care must be taken not to damage new shoots which may be just under soil level, particularly in the spring. Dig a trench out round the plant, to at least a spade's depth, undercutting the rootball as far as possible with the spade or a trowel. From this point it should be possible to lever the whole clematis out of the hole on to a waiting sheet of polythene or sack. Retain as much soil on the root system as possible, and move it all to the new position. This is usually fairly simple if the new site is in the same garden. However, if this is not the case, and the clematis is likely to be out of the soil for more than an hour or so, it should be placed in a polythene sack with as much of the remaining top growth as possible, and tied in to prevent the roots from drying out. With a large plant in warm weather, a second sack may be required over the top.

Fig 18 'Dawn', one of the first of the large-flowered varieties to bloom. This one will fade if it is grown in full sun.

Replanting should be much easier. Basically you should follow the instructions given on pages 19–24, but prepare a hole commensurate with the size of the plant. The surrounding soil must be kept moist at all times during the first spring and summer after the move.

The large-flowered hybrids are the easiest to re-establish. The montanas generally become too big and woody after a season or two, whilst the other fibrous-rooted varieties, such as the *alpina* and *orientalis* types, tend to lose so much root in the process that they do not take to a move readily.

CHAPTER 3

Pruning

'Pruning is really a matter of common sense.' Faced with that statement and an untidy mass of apparently dead twigs which are only recognisable as clematis by the label, the gardener with little experience may well think that this chapter will be of no help to him. However, if he has no preconceived ideas about what to do, he may be the easiest to help. Given a series of instructions, it is very easy for the gardener simply to do as he is told, and to stop looking and thinking about his plants for himself. This chapter sets out to list a series of guidelines to help establish the plants. Once that has been done, the pruning regime can be modified according to the situation you have chosen and the weather conditions pertaining to your area to get the best results.

PRUNING A NEW CLEMATIS

Regardless of its future pruning type, the newly-planted clematis should be cut back to about 12in (30cm) in height during its first spring. By pruning each stem in this way to just above two good buds, two new stems will be encouraged to grow from each of the existing stems, thus providing a multi-stemmed framework for the future. A clematis should not be allowed to grow away on just one or two stems. The loss of a few flowers in the first spring is a small price to pay for doubling the plant's flowering potential in seasons to come.

BASIC PRUNING

There are a number of groups into which clematis can be divided for pruning purposes, the complexities of which, particularly in the hybrid varieties, can be something of a minefield. It is therefore advisable in the first instance to follow Christopher Lloyd's advice in *Clematis* (Viking 1989) for 'the busy man who has not the time to go into the whys and wherefores', and apply three basic pruning methods:

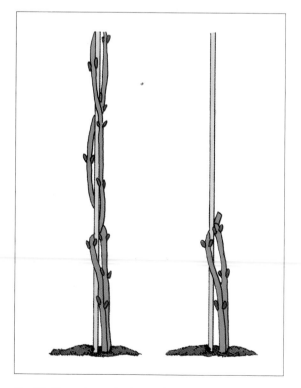

Fig 19 Clematis cut back to 12in (30cm) the first spring after planting.

Group 1 Clematis that flower in the spring need to be pruned only if space is limited. They flower on their old wood (that is, the growth they have made the previous season), so, when it is necessary to prune this group, old stems that have flowered should be cut back in early summer when flowering has finished. This will enable subsequent new growth to ripen during the remainder of the summer, ready for flowering the next spring. These new stems can be tied back to their support as necessary. Varieties in this group include *C. alpina*, *C. macropetala*, *C. montana* and its varieties, and *C. armandii*.

Group 2 This group includes clematis that flower on short stems produced from the previous season's old wood. These are the early large-flowered hybrids, the double and semi-double hybrids, and the mid-season hybrids which normally have their first flowers before the end of June. As they flower on their old wood, pruning is essentially light. Towards the end of February or the beginning of March, when the weather conditions are favourable, remove any dead or weak stems. A word of caution: do trace any apparently dead stems through from the bottom of the plant to the top, before severing low down – many which look dead near the base support vines which have flowering buds higher up that may not be immediately apparent. Remaining stems should be shortened back to just above the top pair which, at that time of year, will be fat and green; it is from these buds that the flowering shoots will develop. Stems should be tied in to their supports as they are cut back. These varieties can eventually become rather bare at the base, and at such time benefit from being pruned back to about 12in (30cm) after their first flowering. Varieties in this group include 'Miss Bateman', 'Nelly Moser', 'Vyvyan Pennell', 'Duchess of Edinburgh', and 'General Sikorski'.

Group 3 Clematis that *only* flower late in the season (that is, after the middle of June and well into the autumn), flower only on their new wood, and the previous season's growth is unwanted. Pruning involves cutting back all the previous year's growth to just above a good pair of buds some 10–12in (25–30cm) from the ground. Over the years, a not inconsiderable stump of greyish-brown stems will form from which the new stems will arise, but hard pruning will also encourage new stems to emerge from below soil level. It is most important that pruning does not take place any earlier than the end of February or the beginning of March, although at that time it may well be necessary to discard many healthy green shoots that have been growing well for many weeks. The British climate can be very fickle and pruning too early can result in the new buds in the leaf axils starting into growth too soon, only to be damaged by severe weather conditions later in the spring. Varieties in this group include the

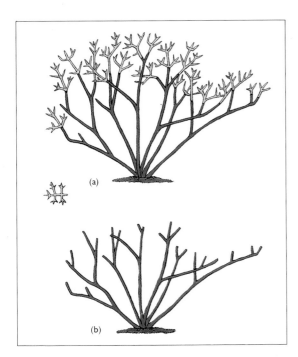

Fig 20 (a) Dead or weak stems, the previous year's flowering stems, cut back to a pair of fat buds. (b) Group 2 clematis after light pruning in February or early March.

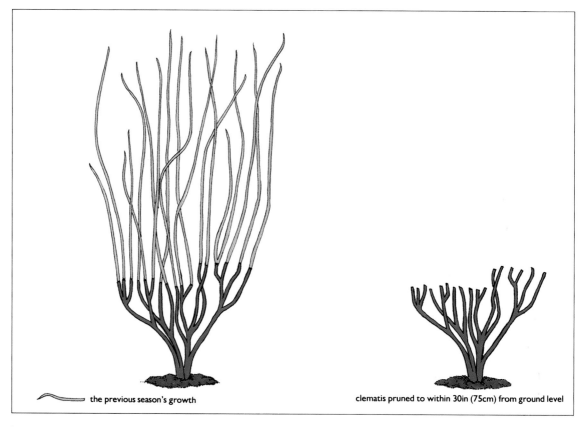

the previous season's growth

clematis pruned to within 30in (75cm) from ground level

Fig 21 Group 3 clematis flower on the new season's growth. The old vines are removed by cutting back to a strong pair of buds.

hybrids such as 'Jackmanii', 'Rouge Cardinal' and 'Hagley Hybrid', the viticellas, and *vitalba*. The texensis group will, like the herbaceous clematis, normally die back to ground level leaving just the dead wood to be removed. The *tangutica* and *orientalis* types can be generally included under this heading, although in practice these are often cut back to about half their height.

Breaking or Bending the Rules

Rules have to be understood before they can be broken. When the gardener observes and so begins to understand his clematis, he can employ pruning techniques to suit his requirements. There is great scope for experimentation, particularly with the early and mid-season large-flowered hybrids, most of which will flower on both old and new growth.

The relationship between time of flowering and time of pruning has to be grasped or accidents will occur – they may not be fatal, but they will cause disappointments for that year. For example, the result of an over-concise magazine article instructing readers to prune clematis in February can be a rash of non-flowering montanas, no early-flowering hybrids, and no double flowers for the whole year, as these all flower on the previous year's growth. One of our customers 'tidied up' her 'Jackmanii' in June, because it was outgrowing its allotted space, and in so doing removed its flowering potential – she then complained about its lack of bloom! The weather can also be unco-operative, with freezing winds in mid-April

Fig 22 (Opposite) 'Allanah', a variety that requires hard pruning.

30

cutting plants back to ground level and thus effectively eliminating any clematis flower before the end of June, or gales in mid-June mutilating plants and removing many buds, resulting in a disappointing display.

Pruning the varieties included in Group 2 (*see* page 29) is usually recommended to be a 'light tidy up'. This should result in an abundance of large blooms towards the end of May or the beginning of June, plus, for many varieties (provided they are well fed and watered), a second flowering in late August or September. This is the accepted way of dealing with the early-flowered hybrids such as 'Nelly Moser', 'Lasurstern' and 'Barbara Dibley', but there are gardeners who habitually hard prune these varieties together with their Group 3 plants early in the year. This is usually because they like a clean and tidy start to the year, or

because the site does not lend itself to a tangle of dead-looking stems during the winter months. However, it can also be a deliberate attempt to have an abundance of flower later in the year.

The mid-season varieties such as 'Marie Bois-selot', 'Henryi' and 'Kathleen Wheeler' are often described as 'optional pruners'. They exhibit extremely large blooms on their old wood, their late blooms being similar but somewhat smaller. Some people treat these as Group 2, some as Group 3, but it is possible, and in some situations a good idea, to adopt both methods on the one plant. By cutting back half the stems to about 12in (30cm) from the ground, whilst just removing the weak growth on the remainder, some of the very large blooms are produced together with an abundance of later smaller flowers. Additionally (and this could be

Fig 23 A most floriferous variety from Poland, 'General Sikorski'.

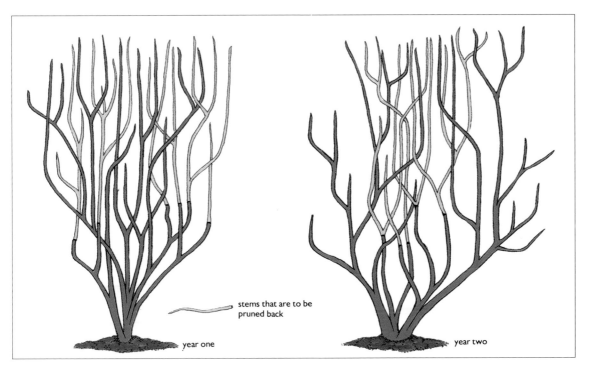

stems that are to be
pruned back

year one

year two

Fig 24 The large-flowered mid-season varieties such as 'Henryi' and 'Marie Boisselot' can become very leggy if they are continually only lightly pruned. Reducing some stems to 30in (75cm) from ground level on alternate years will result in a plant which is well furnished at the base. Stems must only be cut back to a point just above two buds.

more important), by alternating the halves from one year to the next, the plant is rejuvenated from the bottom and prevented from becoming leggy, which is the tendency with these varieties if they are left unpruned.

Some of the Group 3 or hard-pruning types will produce quite large blooms early in the summer if left unpruned and, whilst it is desirable to prune most of the plant hard to prevent the lower growth from becoming unsightly, it can be interesting to leave a few stems unpruned to see if any early flowers are produced. Varieties which work well in this respect are 'Ernest Markham', 'Gipsy Queen', 'Niobe' and 'Ville de Lyon'. These late-flowering varieties can become a most unsightly tangle by the autumn, and it does no harm to cut them back to about 40–60in (100–150cm) high in Novem-

ber as an interim measure, if you need to. The final pruning is then carried out in February or March as usual.

The pruning point of these Group 3 types may be varied after the initial hard pruning in the first year. For example, a clematis grown through a tree may be more suited to a pruning point where the vines reach the first bough rather than nearer the ground, thus obviating the need to retrain the new brittle stems up a supporting wire or cane each year. More than one pruning point may be desirable. For instance, a hard-pruning variety that is to be trained around a window could have several different lengths of stem – some quite short to enable the new vines to be taken straight up the wall, and some considerably longer, providing a permanent framework underneath the window,

33

(a)

(b)

Fig 25 (a) A tall-growing, hard-pruning clematis with two winter pruning points. (b) The new vines are later trained to provide an abundance of summer flowers.

thus enabling new growth to be trained up the wall on the other side.

The way in which the more rampant 'species' varieties are pruned can greatly alter their appearance and the space which they occupy. A *montana* will clamber for 35–50ft (10–15m) through a large conifer or old apple tree, or rampage over outbuildings and fences if left unpruned. However, it can be contained to an area as small as a gate post if it is judiciously pruned. Provided it has been well pruned and tied in from its early years, a *montana* can be pruned back very severely to a bare framework of branches, shortly after flowering early in June. This will allow plenty of time for new growth to develop, be tied in and ripen during the summer and autumn, ready for flowering the following spring. Although less vigorous, the *alpina* and *macropetala* types can be similarly trained after flowering, to keep them in a restricted space.

Usually, the *tangutica* and the *orientalis* types should be pruned hard. However, in a situation where tidiness is not too important, only light pruning in February or March will extend an already lengthy flowering season, with some blossom in June. When grown against a wall, these varieties can be left with a permanent framework attached to trellis or wires, the old growth being removed in early March by shearing the plant as one would the side of a hedge. This is a most satisfactory method of pruning wall-grown *orientalis* types, as it ensures flowers and seed heads from top to bottom, limiting the thickness of the plant as it is cut back so closely to its framework.

For successful results, pruning must go hand in hand with feeding and watering. Varieties that flower on both their old and new wood are often so exhausted after their first magnificent flowering, that without prodigious feeding (a gallon of tomato fertiliser a week is not too much for an established plant), they will not bloom later in the year on their new growth. The aim of pruning is to produce large numbers of good quality flowers on a healthy framework of stems, but it is only possible to achieve this if you make sure the plant is completely happy in other respects.

Pruning the Established Clematis

On moving to a property, the new occupant may be faced with the problem of trying to identify a mass of unlabelled, unattractive, tangled stems in the garden, particularly if it is wintertime. Some at that stage will be unidentifiable. Indeed, it often happens that prize examples of mature, and sometimes quite rare, clematis plants are ripped out of the ground, unrecognised by new owners of a property.

So what should he do? On examining the plants, it may be obvious from the array of stumps and cut stems that some have been regularly cut back in the past. It is probable that these will be varieties that are included under our Group 3, and could therefore be pruned with some confidence. Failing this, or if there is doubt, it will be necessary to live with the plants for a year, noting when they flower and feeding them well. It should then be possible to determine their pruning requirements. A general rule is that plants which flower before the end of June are doing so on their old wood and consequently need light pruning only; plants that do not flower until the end of June or later on their new wood require hard pruning in February or March.

Inevitably, there are one or two exceptions to this rule. If the preceding winter has been particularly severe, there is the possibility that the early, large-flowered hybrids, such as 'Nelly Moser', may have been so badly damaged that they have no viable old wood on which to flower in the spring and, in consequence, do not bloom until late summer. Additionally, some of the hard-pruning varieties, such as 'Ernest Markham' or 'Ville de Lyon', may flower in June on their old wood. Many varieties can quite easily be identified from books or from photographs in specialist catalogues.

Rampant montanas present their own problems, creeping under tiles, and blocking both

Fig 26 Clematis orientalis *before pruning.*

Fig 27 The same Clematis orientalis *after pruning.*

36

Fig 28 A tightly pruned Clematis montana *round a cottage window.*

gutters and doorways. Severe cutting back with a pair of shears will often be sufficient to clear gutters and doorways – this can be undertaken at any time from spring through to late autumn without endangering the plant. However, it must be remembered that flowering the following spring may be minimal if pruning was carried out late in the year. Occasionally, much more drastic pruning – cutting back to the last 3½ft (1m) or so of stem – is necessary. In this event (which should be avoided if at all possible), there is a high risk that the whole plant will be killed. The shock to the plant is obviously very great and there may be no dormant buds from which it can rejuvenate itself. Sometimes a few new shoots will start into growth only to subsequently collapse and die. It is a frustrating fact that if you want a *montana* to survive, it won't; if you try to kill it, you can't! *Alpina* and *macropetala* do not take kindly to drastic treatment either, whereas *tangutica* and *orientalis* will frequently survive.

With hybrids it is fairly safe to say that, unless the plant has been regularly pruned throughout its life, it may well not have any viable buds still alive on the lower part of its stem. Therefore, even if it is a variety which should normally be hard pruned, an old established plant should only be pruned back to the lowest pair of good buds on each stem. This may result in a plant that is very bare and unattractive at the bottom. To overcome this, it may be possible to train some of the stems towards the ground where they may even be encouraged to layer (*see* page 92 on propagation), and eventually send up new growth from the base.

Some of the most impossible 'bird's nests' occur when the early large-flowered varieties have been left unpruned and untrained for some years. The tendrils cling to the nearest stem, resulting in a mass of dead wood and plant debris encased in a network of vines which can become more than 3½ft (1m) deep. Instead of presenting an array of flat faces, the flowers become strangled. Something has to be done, and there are two possible courses of action. If time is short, cut back the mass of stems from the top, carefully looking for the lowest two buds and making that a pruning point. All plant debris and weak stems should be removed and the shortened stems must be spread out and tied back immediately. If this work is undertaken in February or March, the early flowers on such varieties as 'Dr Ruppel' and 'H. F. Young' will of course be lost, but there should be the compensation of a good show in late summer. If this pruning is done later in the year, the plants are unlikely to flower again until the following year.

A much more time-consuming method is to shear off the top 12in (30cm) or so of any material that is hanging down and then painstakingly remove the plant from its support, vine by vine. This can only be done by cutting through the tendrils that hold the stems together with a pair of secateurs – it is tedious work and inevitably some of the stems will get broken. These broken stems must then be shortened back to a good pair of buds low down on the stem. This will in fact improve the plant as it will help refurbish the bottom with new growth. The need to feed plants that have received any form of drastic treatment must be emphasised if a vigorous, floriferous clematis is to be attained.

CHAPTER 4

Climate and Aspects

A cold, still New Year's Day brought a customer to our nursery. He had travelled some distance with some friends to look round, and complained bitterly that the display of flowers he had seen growing outside the previous June was nowhere to be found! According to him, we had no business advertising the nursery when there was nothing to be seen!

Fortunately, such misunderstanding is rare, but, although some clematis can be seen in flower for much of the year, inexperienced gardeners do expect plants to behave like clockwork, regardless of situation, season, weather or latitude. Occasionally, clematis have some flowers early in January, but this would only happen if the winter was mild, and if the previous season had co-operated by producing suitable wood on which these early-flowering varieties could bloom. There can also be the odd large-flowered variety, the last of the previous season's blooms hanging on until the inevitable frost and snowfall finishes them off. Such blooms are more objects of curiosity than beauty, often very green in colour, and suffering from the attentions of earwigs as soon as they open. In the lists of varieties included in this book, flowering times and preferred aspects are given, but they should only be used for guidance and then related to the weather pattern in a particular year, and the precise situation of the garden. Overall temperatures, hours of sunshine, amounts of rain, day lengths and likely first and last frosts will vary from one area to another, and even within the garden itself there are warmer and cooler positions. The garden's height above sea level and the configuration of the local landscape also play a part in determining when your clematis is

going to flower and how long its flowering period is likely to last.

As well as considering the various characteristics of any specific garden, thought must also be given to the ancestry of the clematis to be grown there. Many of today's varieties owe their existence to plants that are from many different parts of the world, and the characteristics of many of the wild clematis, which may have originated in countries as far apart as New Zealand, China, or the Himalayas, are passed down, either directly or through hybridisation, into these varieties. It follows that a variety whose origins can be traced back to the warmth of the Mediterranean may need a much more sheltered spot in the UK than one whose ancestors began life half-way up a mountain. This leads us to the most fundamental consideration when buying a new clematis: what variety will suit the precise conditions of a chosen site, or what conditions are called for in order that a specific variety will flourish?

When consulting the list of varieties given in this book or in a nursery catalogue, consider 'aspect' in relation to the section on walls, pages 40–48. Flowering times are shown to enable readers to understand the general habit of the plant – whether it flowers once or twice a year – and to help in planning a succession of flowers over a period. A variety flowering, for example, in May, June and September might, in a good spring, be seen in flower in late April, if it is growing in a sheltered London garden. In the same year, it may not flower until June in a frost pocket in east Scotland. A warm May preceded by a cold April can mean that the *alpina* and *macropetala* types, some montanas and one or two of the early-flowering hybrids can all be seen flowering together; this is unusual in the UK, but normal where there is a short season, as in Norway and Sweden.

It is this unpredictability which makes gardening so interesting. Each year is unique, and no plant looks quite the same from one year to the next. Without the incentive and challenge of creating something new each season, gardening would be repetitive and far less worthwhile.

CLEMATIS AND WALLS, AND THEIR ASPECTS

Clematis have a remarkable capacity to provide colour and height in a confined space, as can be seen in minute London gardens, where the lack of space is outweighed by the benefits of a cloistered position. Apart from the variations of climate dependent upon the geographical considerations, wind is also a major problem for clematis growers. All gardeners have to contend with prevailing south-westerlies, and in coastal districts salt-laden winds create additional difficulties. Clematis do not mind a salt-laden wind, but they do object to being battered to pieces by gales, so they must be planted in the lea of buildings or other shelter in coastal areas. New housing estates lack the natural windbreaks provided by established trees and hedges; wind funnels occur between houses, creating eddies which swirl around in areas confined by house walls and close-boarded fences. These gardens present conditions very different from those in mature town gardens, or in the surprisingly sheltered gardens that have been created in quite open countryside by the planting of shelter belts and hedges.

Clematis are hardy in that, when not in flower, they will survive temperatures well below freezing for quite some time, and if damaged, they will regenerate new growth, provided they have been properly planted. However, frost pockets can cause problems. They are created by cold air, which is denser

Fig 29 A native of China, Clematis armandii. *This variety needs a warm, sheltered spot to do well outside in the UK, but will be successful in a cold greenhouse.*

than warm air, rolling down a slope and collecting in a hollow at the bottom. Gardeners living in such a situation should select their varieties of clematis with care, as the early-summer-flowering hybrids produce their first flush of bloom on growth made the previous year. Of the early-flowering varieties, the alpinas and macropetalas are fairly resistant to frost damage, but the most appropriate choice would be the hard-pruning varieties which flower on their new wood. Even if these are cut back a little, they will still be able to produce enough flowering wood to bloom at the appropriate time.

Hours of sunlight and numbers of frost-free days can also have a bearing on choice when you are considering some of the very early or very late-flowering varieties. For example, unless a

40

favourable micro-climate is known to exist in a certain part of the garden, the early-flowering evergreen variety, *C. armandii*, would not be suitable for an area habitually subjected to late spring frosts. It would survive, but would be unlikely ever to flower. Similarly, 'Lady Betty Balfour', which blooms in September and October, would not suit northern areas of the UK where the winter frosts are earlier.

Adverse conditions can make the advice on suitability of aspect for particular varieties somewhat misleading. The suggestion that a plant will grow in an east- south- or west-facing position, or that another will survive in 'any' aspect, is made on the basis of fairly reasonable conditions in the garden. It should be remembered that the height of a wall and the proximity of other walls can alter considerably the amount of available sunshine and shade. A south-facing wall can in fact be an unsuitable one for a variety requiring a good deal of sunshine, if that area of wall is in the shadow of a tree or another building for much of the day. Also, walls seldom run due north, south, east or west. Conditions need to be considered as sunny or shady, sheltered or exposed, and combinations thereof, and this special knowledge used to vary the information found in catalogues and here.

(In discussing the suitability of walls facing in particular directions for different varieties of clematis, the word 'wall' is used to describe house walls, and garage walls, as well as boundary walls and fences.)

North-Facing Walls

There are north walls and north walls. The difference in climate is great between a north wall taking the full blast of a north-easterly wind from Siberia across an expansive field in Lincolnshire, and one in a courtyard in the Cotswolds.

The only clematis that would survive fairly inhospitable conditions are the montanas, alpinas and macropetalas. The true *montana* types, that is *montana*, *montana rubens* and *montana*

'Elizabeth', are much hardier than the related types such as *chrysocoma* and *vedrariensis*. The alpinas and macropetalas which bloom in April and May are all extremely hardy, but, as with any early spring flowers, they can sustain damage from a late frost. Both *C. alpina*, which originates from Northern Europe, and *C. macropetala* (from the mountainous areas of southern Asia), are subject to temperatures well below freezing in their normal environment. The typical colour of the nodding, bell-shaped flowers is blue, and there are some excellent cultivars, including *C. alpina* 'Pamela Jackman', *C. alpina* 'Frances Rivis', and *C. macropetala* 'Maidwell Hall'. Good pink varieties are *C. macropetala* 'Markham's Pink', *C. macropetala* 'Rosy O'Grady' and *C. alpina* 'Willy', as well as the dusky reddish-purple *C. alpina* 'Ruby'. White cultivars are numerous: *C. alpina* 'Burford White', *C. macropetala* 'White Moth' (double), and *macropetala* 'White Swan', 'White Lady', and 'Snowbird', to name but a few. Two recent macropetalas from Sweden, 'Jan Lindmark', and 'Anders', are mauve, and have provided a very significant development in the colour range.

The large-flowered cultivars most able to

Fig 30 Clematis macropetala *'Jan Lindmark'*.

withstand the rigours of early spring winds are varieties that need to be hard pruned and will therefore be flowering on their new growth. Comparatively short-growing varieties that would be suitable are the two pinks, 'Comtesse de Bouchaud' and 'Hagley Hybrid'. Growing to a height of 17½ft (5m) or so, 'Jackmanii', 'Perle d'Azur' or 'Victoria' would be a good choice for many regions, although they may not do well in the north of the UK. A reasonably sheltered north wall offers much greater scope. Many of the early-summer-flowering hybrids would be suitable. A shady position is a positive advantage for the striped pink or mauve varieties, which otherwise fade so badly in a sunny position. It is also ideal for the lovely pale creamy-yellow 'Wada's Primrose' and the pale pink 'Dawn', both of which quickly fade to white if grown in a less shady situation. Most of the blue clematis tend to prefer a sunny position, but three lavender-blue ones that do well in the shade are 'Alice Fisk', 'Mrs Cholmondeley' and 'William Kennett'. An old favourite that will do quite well is 'The President', with its deep violet-blue flowers. Due to the comparative cold of north wall situations, the early flowering white varieties, 'Duchess of Edinburgh' and 'Miss Bateman', have a tendency towards rather green flowers. Other white varieties, 'Marie Boisselot', 'Henryi' and 'John Huxtable' all do well on a north wall.

Provided that there is good light, many clematis will thrive even with little or no sunlight, but the red varieties do need sunshine if they are to flower and therefore should not normally be considered for a north wall situation. If, however, you have a little sun and are determined to try a red, 'Mme Edouard André' or the two viticellas, 'Kermesina' and 'Mme Julia Correvon' might be worth trying. Of course, if the wall is only about 7ft (2m) high, any number of the tall-growing varieties would succeed, growing up the north side of the wall to flower in the sunlight on the wall top and down the other side.

Varieties Suitable for a North Wall

In exposed conditions:
  C. montana
  C. montana 'Elizabeth'
  C. montana rubens
  C. montana 'Picton's Variety'
In more favourable conditions:
  Above varieties and all *montana*, *alpina* and *macropetala* types
  'Comtesse de Bouchaud'
  'Hagley Hybrid'
  'Jackmanii'
  'Perle d'Azur'
  'Victoria'
Sheltered conditions:
  All above varieties
  'Alice Fisk'
  'Barbara Jackman'
  'Bee's Jubilee'
  'Beauty of Richmond'
  'Carnaby'
  'Dawn'
  'Dr Ruppel'
  'Duchess of Edinburgh'
  'Henryi'
  'Horn of Penty'
  'Joan Picton'
  'John Huxtable'
  'Lincoln Star'
  'Marcel Moser'
  'Miss Bateman'
  'Mrs Cholmondeley'
  'Nelly Moser'
  'Ramona'
  'Richard Pennell'
  'Scartho Gem'
  'Sealand Gem'
  'The President'
  'Wada's Primrose'
  'William Kennett'

Fig 31 'Wada's Primrose' – the nearest to yellow in the large-flowered varieties, it retains its colour if it is planted in a light but shady position.

South-Facing Walls

'It should have been all right. It was a lovely south-facing wall, it had its head in the sun and I did put some pebbles round to shade the roots.' So often we hear customers ask why, if they did all this, something went wrong. Certainly, most clematis will gravitate towards the sun, however, many will do very well without a great deal of sunshine. The essential prerequisite for a flourishing clematis is a rich, moist soil, and this is rarely to be found against a south wall. A sun-baked border, perfect for pinks, rosemary and lavender, is not ideal for clematis, but they will survive, provided that care is taken when planting and that constant attention is given to watering during dry spells of weather. Most clematis that fail, or produce only stunted growth, do so because of an inadequate supply of water and nutrients.

There are some varieties which, having been well planted and nurtured through the first year or two, will survive in conditions alien to their normal requirements. It is often the species and small-flowered clematis that will withstand a degree of ill-treatment. We know of a good example of this in Lincolnshire, where a *montana* type, *C. spooneri*, and a 'Marie Boisselot' (climbing through a 'Zephirine Drouhin' rose) were growing on a south-facing wall. As the garden became neglected, the *spooneri* survived, giving a good display of bloom each spring, while the 'Marie Boisselot' declined, and eventually gave up altogether with lack of adequate sustenance. Although the montanas grow very vigorously in moist soil, they are usually extremely floriferous once they get established in a dry, sunny spot. Their fibrous root system seems to be able to extract more moisture from the soil than the more linear roots associated with the large-flowered hybrids can. Although the delicate cut-leafed foliage is much more sparse, the yellow bell-shaped flowers of *tangutica* and the *orientalis* types do not seem to suffer, their fibrous root system again serving them well.

Viticella and its cultivars will also survive, once established, on fairly dry soil, as will *C. flammula*, the late-flowering scented variety that can be found growing wild in Provence in France. Sometimes this lives on the most impoverished-looking limestone shale, its deep roots obviously finding nutrient and moisture somewhere below, sustaining it during the extreme summer heat punctuated by the occasional violent thunderstorm.

When considering the problem of drought that can be associated with south-facing walls, it should be remembered that fences and trellis work are not usually affected in this way. The water falls on the north side of the fence, easily soaking through to the south side, unless the lie of the land prevents this. A brick wall's normal tendency is to absorb moisture from the soil, no matter which way it faces, and this, coupled with the effect of the sun, which encourages more water absorption as well as reflecting heat back on to the soil itself or the vegetation growing there, means that any plant situated there will need more water.

As long as adequate moisture levels can be maintained, both the reflected and retained warmth of the wall can be of tremendous benefit for some of the more tender species of climbers. Many would-be purchasers of evergreen clematis seem to want the plant in order to cheer up a dreary, north-facing wall or fence, but such a situation is quite inappropriate for this type of clematis, which needs all the warmth it can get. There are essentially two evergreen varieties that will grow outside in reasonably favourable areas of the UK, the most sought-after of which is *C. armandii*, a native of central and western China. It has long dark green leaves, somewhat reminiscent of bamboo, and in early spring simple white or blush-white highly-scented flowers which are borne in clusters. Unfortunately, like some of the montanas, there are a number of poor clones of *C. armandii* on the market. It is important to buy this type from a reliable source, or buy one of the named cultivars like 'Apple Blossom' or 'Snow Drift'. Not only does *C. armandii* benefit from the

Fig 32 C. cirrhosa *needs a warm wall if it is to flower well.*

warmth of a south wall, but it also needs to be planted in a sheltered position, as wind damage can turn the leaves to a very unattractive leathery brown. In many districts, it is more suited to growing in a conservatory or cold greenhouse.

Rather more robust foliage is displayed by the other group of evergreen clematis that are sufficiently hardy for outside cultivation. These come from the Balearic Islands and other Mediterranean regions, and will be found variously named in catalogues as *C. balearica*, *C. cirrhosa var. balearica*, *C. calycina syn.* '*Balaerica*', and so on depending on the region of the Mediterranean from which the original plants came. Although they all have a similar habit, and to the inexperienced they may all look very much the same, there are differences which are important to the connoisseur. They all have finely-cut, evergreen leaves which turn a bronzy colour in the winter, but this foliage can vary considerably, in that some leaves are more fleshy and some more finely toothed than others. They all have small creamy-white, pendulous flowers, many having little reddish-purple freckles within the open mouth of their bell, and the size and numbers of these vary from variety to variety. Depending on conditions, they bloom from January through to March and perhaps into April where it is cold. Being vigorous they can cover quite an expanse of wall, but they will only bloom satisfactorily if the wood on which they are to flower has been thoroughly ripened in the sunshine during the previous summer.

Two delicate clematis, *C. florida* 'Sieboldii' (or *C. florida* 'Bicolor', as it is often known), and *C. florida* 'Alba Plena' are currently in great demand. They need a sheltered south or south-west corner to do well. They are more difficult than many varieties to propagate so there is a scarcity value and, as they can also be difficult to cultivate, there is a high failure rate! Both have fragile-looking stems, and pretty flowers, which appear in late June or early July through to August. *C. florida* 'Sieboldii' is often likened to the passion flower, with its outer ring of white sepals framing a central boss of a mass of fiery purple, petal-like stamens. An unusual feature of the flower is that the central rosette remains long after the outer sepals have fallen. *C. florida* 'Alba Plena' is less showy, but perhaps more beautiful. The outer ring of white sepals surrounds concentric rings of greenish-white stamens.

Provided that they can obtain sufficient moisture and a cool root run, many clematis can be grown in a south-facing position, but most would do equally well if facing east or west. However, there are some, particularly the fairly late-flowering red varieties such as 'Ernest Markham' and 'Ville de Lyon', which do require a sunny position, although a due south aspect would not be essential, except in northern districts of the UK. The very late-flowering 'Lady Betty Balfour', a vivid blue-purple flower, most certainly needs a south wall if it is to bloom in September and October. In fact, it may well be a non-starter further north than the Humber. Other late-summer-flowering varieties, such as the rich purple 'Gipsy Queen' and the dusky purple 'Mme Grange', also need the maximum amount of sunshine and a site that is unlikely to be caught by early frosts. Generally speaking, the later the variety flowers, and the further north you go, the more valuable a south wall.

Varieties that Require a South Aspect

C. armandii	
C. cirrhosa (syn. 'Balearica')	(or sheltered south-west position)
C. florida 'Sieboldii'	
C. florida 'Alba Plena'	

'Lady Betty Balfour'

In northern counties of the UK, all late-flowering hybrids and *C. flammula* need a south-facing wall.

East- and West-Facing Walls

If they are fairly sheltered from the wind, east- and west-facing positions can provide ideal conditions for clematis, as they are not usually as dry as positions facing south. The list of suitable varieties seems almost limitless. The alpinas, macropetalas and montanas would provide early flower, whilst the other late-flowering species clematis would bloom in late summer. Between these two ends of the season, the large-flowered hybrids can provide a continuity of colour, the choice of variety depending on the amount of sunshine or shade a particular site has to offer. With the exception of those varieties that must have a south-facing site, virtually any type of clematis can be considered and related to the site to be used.

Some varieties are worth a mention. The 'blues' immediately come to mind – 'H. F. Young', raised by Walter Pennell of Lincoln, is one of the earliest of the hybrids. It is a well-rounded mid-blue flower and has the advantage of being a variety which blooms well from the bottom of the plant. Another early compact-growing variety is 'Alice Fisk', described as wisteria-blue, not a pure colour but contrasting well with the dark brown stamens. This was Jim Fisk's cross between two excellent blue clematis, 'Lasurstern' (which has similarities to 'H. F. Young'), and 'Mrs. Cholmondeley'. 'Will Goodwin' is a slightly later pale lavender-blue variety with crenulated edges to its sepals. Of the deeper blues, 'Elsa Spath' is excellent for a small garden, whilst the more rugged-looking 'Lord Nevill' makes an altogether larger plant. 'General Sikorski' was a welcome variety from Poland, introduced by Jim Fisk in 1980. It has mid-blue sepals and golden stamens, and flowers abundantly through June, July and August. Poland has produced some excellent clematis over the past ten years or so: 'Niobe', with its dark ruby-red velvety sepals, fast became a firm favourite, and two more recent introductions are the bright crimson 'Cardinal Wyszynski' and 'Warsaw Nike', a royal-velvet purple. Both are extremely free-flowering clematis, blooming from June to September.

The double varieties perhaps respond best to a sheltered west or south-westerly direction, and their large double heads in May and June are usually followed by single flowers in August and September. 'Vyvyan Pennell' is the most popular of this group, but there are many others which are equally rewarding, some more fully double than others. As yet the double red is still elusive, but some very worthwhile introductions have been made in the past few years. 'Glynderek' and 'Royalty' are much deeper blues than the lovely 'Beauty of Worcester' and the old favourite, the pale blue 'Countess of Lovelace'. 'Kathleen Dunford', a rosy-purple semi-double, is considerably deeper in colour than the others in the pink

Fig 33 The full double flowers of 'Belle of Woking'.

Fig 34 'Dorothy Walton'.

range – 'Walter Pennell', 'Proteus' and 'Mrs Spencer Castle'. 'Sylvia Denny', a pure white, is similar to the 'Duchess of Edinburgh', but does not have the same tendency towards green sepals, so could in some ways be considered an improvement. There is, nevertheless, a certain charm about these greenish flowers, and the most unusual of all must be 'Belle of Woking'. The lime-green buds gradually open to reveal a fully double flower of a pale silver-grey. 'Belle of Woking' is a variety that always provokes an opinion – either loved or loathed!

There are some extremely good rosy-pinks and mauves that do not fade badly, as do their striped counterparts. 'Horn of Plenty' and 'Kathleen Wheeler' can both have very large blooms of about 8in (20cm) in diameter, while 'Richard Pennell' and 'Ruby Glow' are a little smaller. Size isn't everything, and for a slightly less favourable

site, the 4–5in (10–12cm) rosy-mauve flowers of 'Sealand Gem' will cover quite an extensive area from June to September. If this variety is pruned by cutting the stems back to various lengths, it will cover a wall or fence from top to bottom. Two hard-pruning, very free-flowering varieties are 'Dorothy Walton' and 'Twilight'. 'Dorothy Walton' is a vigorous grower to about 17½ft (5m), and the shape of its long pointed mauve-pink sepals is a complete contrast to the round dusky petunia-mauve flowers of 'Twilight', which makes a very compact plant, growing to 7–10½ft (2–3m).

A sheltered wall with an east- or west-facing aspect has endless possibilities, giving you the chance of having clematis in flower from April through to September and October, or even later.

CHAPTER 5

House and Garden

There is an obvious relationship between house and garden. How much this is enhanced depends on the gardener and what he, as occupier, does to his house. In some cases, harmony is created, while with others the discord is such that the only link between the two is the communicating door. In older properties, where houses were built from local materials, and garden walls were constructed of stone quarried nearby, there was an immediate link between the two. However, with the coming of the railways in the nineteenth century, which meant that brick could be moved over great distances, this link diminished. Modern transport and strange economic realities make it cheaper to transport a material two hundred miles than to use a local alternative, so that now any material can turn up in any part of the country. A new house built in the flat Lincolnshire fens will look similar to one built on the rocky North Wales coastline. This gives the gardener a different and more difficult job in forming a visual whole between house and garden.

PLANTING BY WALLS

With older properties there is often a feel of rightness, as if they have been built around particular people, with modifications being done, with similar materials, to meet the changing requirements of the owners. Nowadays, domestic architecture is more about economics than personal requirements, with builders putting up properties with scant regard for what is already there. Exceptions to this are to be applauded, but they do tend to be the exception rather than the rule.

Within this context, the clematis and other climbing plants have a great deal to contribute in forming links and breaking that hard line that can divide house from garden, but the gardener has

Fig 35 'Sealand Gem' growing outside a stone cottage in south Lincolnshire.

to be cautious. While many such plants can cover that which we would rather not see, they can equally effectively obscure that of which the architect could be justly proud. Completely covering beautiful brick or stonework with a plant which, during winter months, can hardly be called attractive is not a good idea. On the other hand, the twigs and stems of a *montana* in winter could delight the eye when seen against some modern brickwork.

Many older properties have existing wall shrubs framing the windows and doorways which would provide an ideal host for clematis to clamber through. Many people use clematis in isolation against a wall, but they are sociable plants and enjoy the company of other climbers and wall shrubs. Old fruit trees, magnolias, wisterias, ceanothus, cotoneasters, and so on, make a particularly good support for the very large, summer-flowering varieties such as 'Henryi', 'Fairy Queen' and 'Beauty of Richmond', which have an open habit and can ramble amongst a host. The double and semi-double cultivars also benefit from being grown in this way. A wall-trained shrub should be planted for at least two years (much longer for a slow-growing type), before it can support a clematis.

The appearance of clematis on walls in winter does need to be considered before planting. Remember that clematis do not cling to a wall in the same way as *Parthenocissus quinquefolia* (Virginia Creeper), which has small suckers on the end of each tendril enabling it to adhere to any surface. Most clematis attach themselves by twisting their leaf stalks (petioles) around their support, and it is the nature of this support and its relationship to the building, which have to be carefully considered by the gardener. One answer to the unsightly appearance of clematis in the winter is to plant only hard-pruning varieties in such situations. These can be provisionally cut back to about 3–5¼ft (1–1½m) high in the autumn, giving the advantage of a splendid display of flower in the summer, and stems contrasting with the geometry of the brickwork in winter.

The height of a wall needs to be taken into consideration when choosing a clematis. If a large expanse of wall needs to be covered, a *montana* variety is ideal, but it will require a strong support (*see* Chapter 9). Depending on how it is trained, one *montana* could cover an area of 20–28ft (6–8m) wide and up to the eaves of the house, and, additionally, could be grown on a draughty north-facing wall. A similar density of cover could be achieved by planting some of the vigorous summer-flowering varieties, such as *C. fargesii var.* 'Soulei', *C. orientalis* or *C. tangutica* in a more favourable aspect. Apart from the *montana* types, there is rather a dearth of tall-growing early-flowering clematis. 'John Paul II' has creamy-white flowers and is a vigorous grower to about 17½ft (5m); slightly later, flowering in June, are 'William Kennett', 'Marie Boisselot' and 'Henryi'. Another tall grower with unusually light green foliage is 'Jackmanii Alba', which has almost ragged, bluish-white sepals. The main crop is of single flowers, but there will be some early double flowers if it is only pruned lightly. It is the late-flowering cultivars, such as 'Ernest Markham', 'Gipsy Queen', 'Jackmanii Superba', 'Lady Betty Balfour', 'Mme Baron Veillard', 'Margaret Hunt', 'Perle d'Azur' and 'Victoria', that can offer vigour, height and an abundance of flower, given the right situation. These summer-flowering clematis are so prolific with their flowers that, properly trained and tied in, they can cover a wall with a mass of bloom similar to that provided by the montanas. There are excellent examples of this meticulous training to be seen at Sissinghurst Castle in Kent. On a very large wall, a number of plants of the same variety should be used, spaced approximately 5¼ft (1·5m) apart to give good coverage. Alternatively, one plant could be layered along a wall over a number of years to give the same effect.

Low walls, garage walls, and so on, up to 8¾ft (2·5m) in height can be clothed in clematis from April through to late summer, so wide is the choice of comparatively short-growing varieties

Fig 36 (Opposite) 'Perle d'Azur' growing at Sissinghurst, Kent.

Fig 37 'Snow Queen', an excellent short-growing variety.

and cultivars. The alpinas and macropetalas look good tumbling down retaining and other low garden walls, whilst a *montana* trained along such a wall can give the appearance of a flowering hedge in spring.

The colour of the actual wall is an important consideration when choosing clematis. Some red brick is very harsh and, unless they are grown with other climbers which have bright or light-coloured foliage, the lovely soft mauves of varieties such as 'Horn of Plenty' and 'Kathleen Wheeler' are lost, as are the reds, particularly 'Niobe', 'Voluceau' and *viticella* 'Mme Julia Correvan'. The reds and strong blues look good against stone walls where the pastel shades are rather ineffectual. Strong colours are also needed for white-painted walls; varieties such as 'Mme Grange' and 'Gipsy Queen', or the dark viticellas, 'Etoile Violette' and 'Royal Velours' (which can be difficult to place because of their depth of colour), look superb against a very light background. Where the hard-pruning varieties are used against a white wall, the type of clematis support needs to be chosen with care as it may be visible for several months of the year.

CLEMATIS WITH ROSES AND OTHER CLIMBERS

Unlike the wall shrubs, which need to be established before they can provide a framework for clematis, other climbers such as honeysuckles and roses can be planted together with clematis. However, the vigour of the other climber needs to be investigated first – for instance, nothing can compete with a Russian Vine, *Polygonum baldschuanicum*, which seems to grow as fast as its other name, 'A Mile a Minute', suggests, and will swamp a *montana*.

52

Clematis are gregarious plants; they are very happy to be planted in the same hole as a rose or other climber of modest proportions, deriving enormous benefit from this association. This is particularly the case when they are grown in an open position in the garden, as the clematis then receives some protection from the wind. It appears that many gardeners are now removing their roses in order to replace them with clematis. This is a retrograde step, unless the rose is suffering from some terminal illness. Certainly, old climbing roses do tend to go bare round the knees, revealing unattractive stems, but there are many early-summer-flowering clematis (such as 'Alice Fisk' or 'H. F. Young') that could be used to cover them. The early summer hybrids are also excellent grown in conjunction with the climbing sports of the hybrid tea roses, such as the lovely scented pink 'Caroline Testout', or pillar roses such as 'Golden Showers'. Colour associations, using either strong or pale blues, would be lovely. The pale lavender-blue clematis look wonderful with a very dark red rose such as 'Etoile de Hollande', and a more dramatic contrast with this rose would be a white such as 'Marie Boisselot' or 'Henryi'.

Clematis that do not require a great deal of pruning are more compatible with the pruning requirements of climbing roses. The hard-pruning varieties are more suitable for growing with ramblers, whose pruning would have to be delayed until November when much of the clematis growth could also be cut back. This might offend some tidy-minded rose growers who prefer to prune ramblers immediately after flowering, but it does no harm to the roses. The ramblers are more suited to growing in the open on pergolas or trellis as they are prone to mildew and, because of wind damage, the hard-pruning varieties of clematis are also more suited to such a situation than the earlier flowering cultivars. As both roses and clematis flower in June and July, excellent combinations could be arrived at, particularly if the *viticella* types were included. Some planting associations, such as rose 'New Dawn' with clematis 'Perle d'Azur',

are now very over-worked. Armed with good catalogues of both clematis and roses, the imaginative gardener should be able to arrive at an equally pleasing colour combination.

PERGOLAS, ARCHES AND SCREENS

Pergolas create a three-dimensional feature linking areas of the garden and providing shady walks, the geometry of the structure contrasting with the natural shapes of the plants. A pergola devoted entirely to clematis would be dull, but clematis can make a major contribution to such a planting scheme. The scale and vigour of the climbers used to furnish a pergola must be related to the size of the structure, which can vary from a small-scale wooden framework to large brick and stone-built pillars, with timbers spanning wide paths and substantial borders on either side. There can be different emphases in the planting of a pergola, such as a continuity of interest throughout the year, which might be of paramount importance in a small garden. A predominantly single-colour pergola and surrounding border could be designed either to explode into a comparatively short but dramatic display of colour in midsummer, or be sustained from early spring right through to the autumn – a glance at the flowering times of the white varieties of clematis would show that they could be in bloom from April or May through to September or October.

On a fairly large pergola, the late-summer-flowering clematis could be grown with scented rambler roses. Alternatively, being shorter, the early-summer-flowering hybrids could be used to cover the uprights of the structure with other more vigorous climbers providing the horizontal cover. If they are planted with other climbers, clematis are to some extent protected from the wind, but they should nevertheless be chosen with care if the pergola is in an exposed position. For example, except in an extremely sheltered southern garden, the evergreen

53

Fig 38 Tall-growing, hard-pruning varieties which have an abundance of
flower at the top are ideally suited to supports that need to be clothed well
above the ground level. (a) Simple metal or rustic arches. (b) Open rustic
screens spanning the garden.

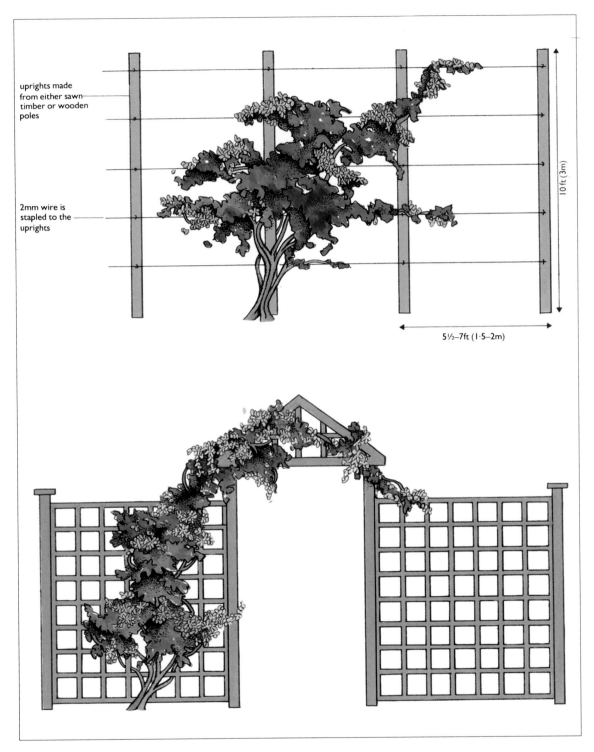

uprights made from either sawn timber or wooden poles

2mm wire is stapled to the uprights

10 ft (3m)

5½–7ft (1·5–2m)

Fig 39 Vertical post sunk into the ground and joined by horizontal wires quickly makes an effective and dense screen when planted with the vigorous species varieties, such as serratifolia, tangutica, and rehderiana.

*Fig 40 A range of large-flowered varieties growing on a fence in Japan.
Their colours look particularly bright against the background of trees.*

C. armandii is not a good subject for such an open construction.

For a simple rustic or metal arch, a late-flowering variety such as 'Jackmanii Superba' or 'Gipsy Queen', planted with a honeysuckle or rose to mask its bare stem, takes some beating, traditional though it may be! A good depth of colour and a great mass of bloom seem to be necessary when framing a gateway or entrance to another part of the garden. A closely-trained *montana* can be used with equal success, but it does have a much shorter flowering season. A series of metal arches can also be used to create a tunnel which would result in a shady walk, similar to a pergola. Various arch shapes and bowers are now being manufactured and these would be ideal for a combination of rambler roses and summer-flowering clematis.

Screens can be both functional and decorative. They can be used to conceal eyesores or create privacy, in which case they need to be fairly densely covered, either with a *montana*, or clematis in conjunction with other climbers such as large-leafed ivies. A simple dividing screen can be made by positioning a series of poles about 7ft (2m) apart, joining them up with horizontal wires, and planting them up with some of the species clematis and honeysuckles, which will soon make excellent cover. Less functional screens, many of which can be extremely decorative structures in their own right, used simply to divide one area of the garden from another, would require lighter planting – the alpinas, macropetalas, viticellas and large-flowered hybrids are more appropriate than the more vigorous species clematis.

CHAPTER 6

Planting into Trees and Shrubs

Much has been written about the desirability of planting clematis to ramble through trees and shrubs. Wonderful combinations are envisaged, and rightly so, because this is the most natural way to grow the plant. *C. vitalba* and *C. flammula* thrive in the hedgerows of the UK and Provence respectively, whilst the large-flowered species clematis, *patens*, flourishes in Japan. In reality, many gardeners experience problems or failures because the relationship between the needs of the tree and those of the clematis are not fully understood. If the tree or shrub is bigger, it will win the battle for nutrients and water, unless a great deal of thought is given to the siting of the plant and to the soil preparation.

HOSTS

In general, mature forest trees such as beech, oak, lime, and so on, do not provide suitable hosts, nor do some of the garden trees – many of the flowering cherries, rowans or crab-apple – because they have too dense a canopy. Having said that, there are always exceptions to the rule, such as a gigantic weeping willow in Lincolnshire festooned with the blossoms of *montana* in May and June. The clematis was planted some distance from the outer limbs of the tree and then trained back on to the tree on a wire. There is plenty of available moisture, and it benefits from the rich fenland soil.

The ideal tree or shrub to host a clematis is one that has a fairly open habit and whose branches are sturdy rather than whippy. Branches that blow about a great deal make it difficult for the clematis to take hold, whilst the continual movement can cause damage to the clematis stem which, in turn, can give access to disease.

It is in many ways easier to plant a clematis into a mature tree, whether deciduous or evergreen, as it has more or less stopped extending its branches, and the limits of its roots are known. In the modern, newly-planted garden, where trees will have to grow for many years before they reach their ultimate size, consideration must be given to future growth if the clematis is not to be quickly overtaken by its host. As the tree roots are likely to extend at least as far out from the trunk as do the branches, it may be necessary to site the clematis some distance from its host, in the knowledge that within a year or two the tree will grow to it. It should be planted on the north or shaded side if possible, in good deep soil that has been properly prepared (*see* page 19). It will be necessary to train the clematis up into the tree by means of a stout cane or wires until its own stem thickens sufficently to support it. Until it becomes established, the new plant will need careful feeding and watering, as initially there will be no real depth of root to sustain it, particularly in periods of dry weather. After a few years in which to become really established, it is likely that, even if the clematis is engulfed beneath the branches of the tree, it

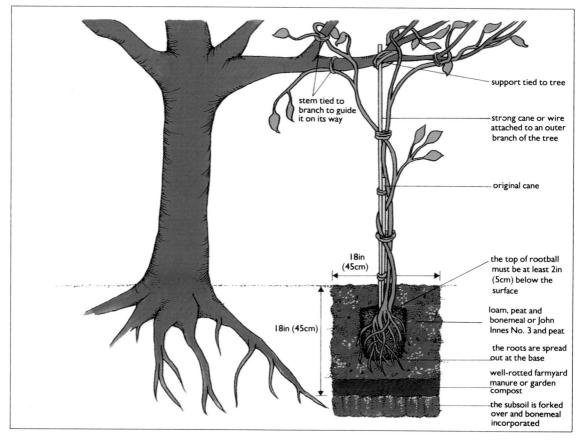

Fig 41 Planting a clematis to the outer branches of a tree, avoiding the tree roots and the canopy.

will still survive and do well. By then it will have a root system large enough to compete with its host, in rather the same way that *C. vitalba* survives in the hedgerow.

WHICH CLEMATIS?

As clematis have almost as many different characteristics and patterns of growth as have the trees into which they are planted, it is necessary to consider the habits of the two in order to achieve a satisfactory planting combination. Varieties chosen to grow into trees do need to be robust and have a certain degree of

vigour if they are to succeed. So often the *montana*, because it has these qualities and is fast growing, is considered to be the answer to tree planting, when clearly it is not. For example, if you were to plant a *montana* through a *Prunus* 'Amanogawa', a tree with a narrow, upright habit flowering in April, within three or four years the *montana* would have made the tree a pole-like support, completely smothering it. More satisfactory would be a hard-pruning variety, such as 'Victoria' or 'Perle d'Azur', which would provide flower to the full height of the tree later in the season, yet would not spoil the delicate pink cherry blossom of the spring.

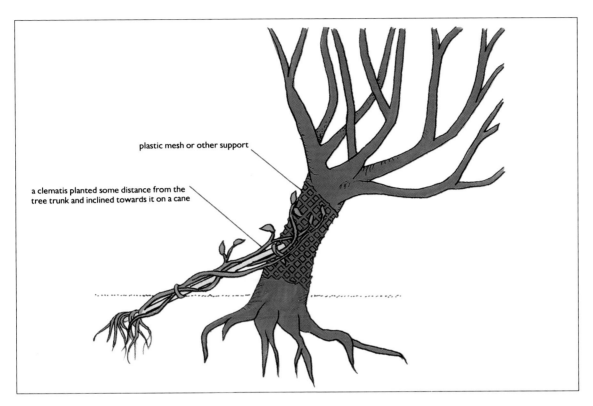

plastic mesh or other support

a clematis planted some distance from the
tree trunk and inclined towards it on a cane

Fig 42 Clematis planted against the trunk of a tree that does not have a large
canopy.

With the exception of badly-mutilated or partially-felled trees, all have some redeeming features or characteristics that need to be preserved. However, some, such as lilac, or *Philadelphus* (Mock Orange), do have distinct drawbacks or limitations, with their comparatively short flowering period and uninteresting foliage for much of the summer. They have little to commend them in July and August and could well benefit from the flowers of a later variety of clematis.

An assessment of the tree and its situation in the garden needs to be made before the clematis is purchased, and the gardener should be quite clear in his mind what he wants that plant to do. Is the clematis required to totally cover the tree? A large apple or pear tree, long past its fruiting best, can make an ideal host for

a *montana*, if the main framework of branches is still strong enough to support what will quickly become a very heavy weight. Many a decaying tree has failed under such a burden! Given four or five years, the tree could be transformed into a cascade of pink or white blossom in May and June.

If the clematis is not required to envelop the host totally, then its virtues need to be examined. Is the tree of value for its fruit, flowers, leaves or generally attractive shape? Consider the flowering time of the tree related to the clematis. Should they bloom at the same time, or would it be advantageous to grow a variety of clematis that would flower earlier or later in the season than the tree?

The tracery of branches and winter silhouette of many trees would be completely ruined by a tangle of old clematis stems, as would the pale pink flowers of the autumn flowering cherry, or *Viburnum bodnantense*. Similarly, the glossy leaves of holly or other evergreens could not be appreciated through a 'bird's nest' of clematis vines. These situations all call for the planting of the hard-pruning hybrids, viticellas or other species clematis. These can be partially cut back to within 3½ft (1m) of the pruning point in late November or December, by which time the old leaves and stems are quite brittle and can easily be removed from the host tree after they have been cut through. The final pruning is then carried out in late February or early March as usual.

Colour

The colour combination of the leaves and flowers of the host tree and those of the clematis which it supports can either be quite subtle, or contrasting and dramatic. Much depends on the gardener's personal choice and what he is trying to do. Colour combinations are very subjective, and opinions vary widely. Gardens open to the public can stimulate ideas, as can the wealth of available gardening books, but it is much more rewarding for the gardener to make his own plant associations, whether deliberately or accidentally. Delightful combinations are often arrived at by chance as the clematis wanders away from its host on to a neighbouring plant. Mistakes will be made, but a young clematis can usually be moved quite successfully in the dormant season (*see* Chapter 2). The desire to create a contrasting or more subtle effect is not only a matter of personal preference, but has to be seen within the context of the particular tree or shrub in the garden, and from what distance it is most frequently to be seen. As an example, the effect of the crimson of 'Ernest Markham' when grown through a purple-leaved tree or shrub might be stunning at close quarters but completely lost when viewed from a distance. As a generalisation, when trying to provide a good tonal contrast, a pale-coloured clematis can be grown into a dark-leaved tree or shrub or vice versa.

Situation

The position of the tree or shrub within the garden, coupled with the prevailing weather conditions, needs to be examined. If the tree is in a fairly exposed position, it is unlikely that the large-flowered hybrids would be successful, as both the early spring growth and subsequent flowers would stand a high chance of being cut back by the wind. Provided the tree was a suitable host, the early-flowering alpinas and macropetalas or perhaps a *montana* could be used, as might also the later-flowering cultivars or species varieties. These smaller-flowered varieties (particularly those which are described as being suitable for 'any aspect') are much more tolerant of windy conditions than are the larger members of the genus. Trees and shrubs in a sheltered garden can, of course, host a much greater range of clematis, but on purely aesthetic grounds, the smaller flowers of the *viticella* cultivars or the late-summer-flowering types look much better in large trees. Whether a clematis is to be grown against a wall or into a tree, the same requirements for sunshine or shade apply. 'Nelly Moser' would fade just as badly when planted into the south side of a shrub as it would beside a sunny front door, whilst a late-flowering variety, such as 'Lady Betty Balfour', would not flower at all growing through a tree receiving little or no sunlight because of the close proximity of buildings. Clematis naturally grow towards the light and sunshine. On a very large tree, they tend to remain on the side on which they were planted, but on a smaller tree they may need some training if they start to grow in the wrong direction. It is also helpful, wherever possible, to plant a clematis in such a way that the prevailing wind takes the vines in the general direction of the tree's branches rather than away from them.

Fig 43 'Victoria' is still very popular more than a century after its first introduction.

Height and Vigour

It follows that the height and vigour of the clematis must be related to the size of the host tree or shrub. Although heights given in catalogues are only approximate, a comparatively short-growing variety, such as the very floriferous 'Hagley Hybrid', which might look splendid growing in a *viburnum*, might do very little more than reach the lowest branches of a 35ft (10m) tree. Tall trees, whether deciduous or evergreen, necessitate a tall-growing clematis, if they are to make any impact. There are some fairly tall-growing mid-season varieties such as 'Fairy Queen', 'Marie Boisselot'. 'W. E. Gladstone' and 'William Kennett'. To get the greatest height, you need the late-summerflowering hybrids and *viticella* cultivars or some of the small-flowered species clematis.

GROWING INTO LARGE TREES

Really large, ancient yew trees or conifers can be wonderful hosts to some of the species clematis, but their situations, with dry and exhausted soil, can often provide some of the most difficult planting conditions. For the first two or three years, particular attention will have to be paid to watering until the clematis has made a deep root system in the good, humus-rich soil that you will have provided when planting. The montanas can usually be persuaded to succeed and, as most will grow to 28–35ft (8–10m) in height, they can clothe a large conifer admirably. There are a number of both pink and white forms of *montana*, some of which are scented. The white *montana* is excellent, as is *chrysocoma sericea*, a close relation of the type, and *montana* 'Alexander', which is

61

Fig 44 C. montana *'Marjorie'*.

both creamy-white and scented, but does need a sunny position if it is to flower well. *Montana* 'Wilsonii' has creamy, twisted sepals, is scented and has the advantage of flowering in June and July, after the other *montana* varieties. (At the time of writing, it is quite difficult to obtain a plant of this variety that is true – unfortunately, many other types of *montana* are sold under this name.)

There are a number of pink montanas and related types, *C. montana rubens* being the best known of these, with its mass of pink flowers in the spring. *C. montana* 'Elizabeth' is a softer pink and is highly scented. Varieties such as *C. montana* 'Tetrarose' and *C. montana* 'Freda' are much deeper in colour and have the added attraction of bronze foliage. A unique variety which was introduced by Jim Fisk in 1980, is *C. montana* 'Marjorie', which is semi-double and is an unusual coppery-pink in colour. Some

montana types are slightly less vigorous than the true *montana* and may, in extreme weather conditions, be less hardy. These include *vedrariensis* and *vedrariensis* 'Highdown'. The deep pink *montana* 'Picton's Variety', can also be very useful, as it is shorter-growing, only reaching a height of some 21ft (6m), but again it can be difficult to obtain correctly labelled.

Montanas, with their profusion of pale, star-like flowers, provide a good contrast to the dark green of *Thuja* and *Cupressus*. However, there are a number of vigorous summer-flowering species that would serve the same purpose, although they are slightly shorter-growing at 17–24ft (5–7m). *C. fargesii* has an abundance of saucer-shaped, 1½in (3cm) white flowers from July through to October. Our native *C. vitalba*, or 'Old Man's Beard', is an excellent variety to climb through large conifers, and its mass of tiny white flowers in July

Fig 45 C. flammula, *highly scented and a native of Provence in France.*

and August, followed by its silky, cream seed heads, are seen to advantage against a dark background. It can grow upwards to about 35ft (10m). *C. flammula* is somewhat similar in appearance, having tiny white scented flowers and silver-grey seed heads, but it is a variety which must have a sunny position if it is to flower successfully. The small-flowered yellow varieties of *C. orientalis* and *C. tangutica*, together with the lemon-scented *C. serratifolia*, all have attractive seed heads and look well against a dark background. All these plants would have a commendable quality when used to clothe a large deciduous tree, such as an old apple, whilst the pink montanas would make an interesting colour combination with the grey or golden forms of *Chamaecyparis* or *Cupressus*.

These small-flowered varieties are worth considering for growing through large trees:

C. montana and all *montana* varieties, including:
C. chrysocoma
C. chrysocoma sericea (syn. spooneri)
C. vedrariensis
C. vedrariensis 'Highdown'

C. apiifolia
C. connata
C. fargesii var. 'Soulei'
C. flammula
C. glauca
C. orientalis and its varieties
C. rehderiana
C. serratifolia
C. tangutica
C. triternata 'Rubro-marginata'
C. vitalba

GROWING INTO MEDIUM-SIZED TREES

For growing into medium to large evergreen and deciduous trees, the selection of varieties from which to choose is much wider. There are numerous light-coloured hybrid and *viticella* cultivars to contrast well with the dark green of yews, hollies, *Thuja* and *Cupressus*. Good mid-season whites are 'Marie Boisselot' and 'Henryi' which flower on both their old and new wood. 'John Huxtable', which is a seedling of 'Comtesse de Bouchaud', is a pure white with yellow stamens, flowers from late June to September, and has all the excellent qualities of hardiness and floriferousness that are found in its parent. 'Huldine' is vigorous, but it does need a sunny position to do well. The quite unusual flowers of *C. viticella* 'Alba Luxurians' are pure white with pale green edges to their sepals; the plant looks superb when growing with a dark green holly. Other varieties that are light in tone, providing a similar contrast with dark foliage, include the pinks such as 'Comtesse de Bouchaud', 'Margaret Hunt', 'Mme Baron Veillard', and the blues of 'William Kennett' and 'Perle d'Azur'. If a mass of smaller flowers is wanted, try the *viticella* cultivars, including 'Abundance', which is rosy-pink, or the paler varieties, 'Little Nell' and 'Minuet'.

The deep-coloured viticellas 'Etoile Violette' and 'Royal Velours' look splendid growing with the golden-leaved conifers or deciduous trees such as *Robinia* 'Frisia'. The well-loved 'Jackmanii' and other summer-flowering hybrids can be used in the same way. Varieties worth considering, are 'Mme Grange', 'Gipsy Queen' and 'Star of India', all deep violets and purples, or the rich crimson 'Ernest Markham'. The pale grey leaves of *Pyrus salicifolia* 'Pendula', the weeping pear, also make a wonderful foil for these rich colours.

Varieties grown into trees must be vigorous – the summer-flowering hard-pruning varieties are generally the most suitable as they have the necessary height and habit of growth. These free-flowering hybrids and viticellas are excellent for enlivening the foliage of laburnum, lilac or cherry long after their flowers have passed. Many of the viticellas are seen at their best against the sky, as they billow from the branches, and some, like 'Huldine', with a pearly-mauve underside to its sepals, can only really be appreciated when viewed from below. 'Victoria', a soft rosy-mauve, and 'Perle d'Azur', which is a sky-blue, also lend themselves to similar treatment.

The montanas are too vigorous for medium-sized trees unless the host tree is to be completely covered, but the macropetalas and alpinas, with their nodding flowers in April and May, followed by their magnificent seed heads, can provide interest in the early part of the year within the branches of a very open tree. They are equally useful for covering a decapitated tree or stump.

Fig 46 C. viticella 'Minuet'.

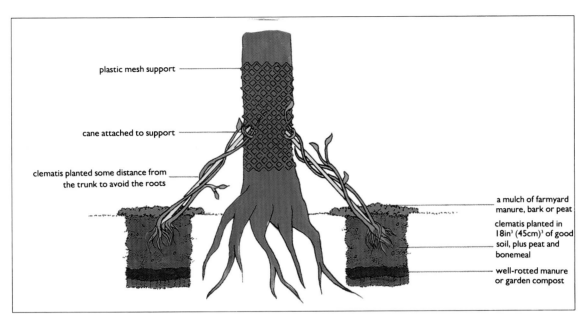

plastic mesh support

cane attached to support

clematis planted some distance from
the trunk to avoid the roots

a mulch of farmyard
manure, bark or peat

clematis planted in
18in³ (45cm)³ of good
soil, plus peat and
bonemeal

well-rotted manure
or garden compost

Fig 47 Two clematis of moderate vigour planted to cover a tall stump. Only
one montana or vigorous species variety would be required.

Varieties worth considering for growing with
medium-sized trees include:

Fig 48 'Alpina Ruby.'

All alpinas and macropetalas
All *C. orientalis* types
C. flammula
C. glauca
C. rehderiana
C. serratifolia
C. triternata 'Rubro-marginata'
C. viticella 'Alba Luxurians'
C. viticella 'Etoile Violette'
C. viticella 'Little Nell'
C. viticella 'Minuet'
C. viticella 'Purpurea Plena Elegans'
C. viticella 'Royal Velours'
C. viticella 'Kermasina'
C. viticella 'Venosa Violacea'
'Comtesse de Bouchaud'
'Dorothy Walton'
'Ernest Markham'
'Gipsy Queen'
'Henryi'
'Huldine'
'Jackmanii'
'Jackmanii Alba'

'Jackmanii Rubra'
'Lady Betty Balfour'
'Lilacina floribunda'
'Marie Boisselot'
'Mme Baron Veillard'
'Mme Grange'
'Mrs Cholmondeley'
'Perle d'Azur'
'Serenata'
'Star of India'
'Victoria'
'William Kennett'

GROWING INTO MEDIUM-SIZED SHRUBS

Medium-sized shrubs, which are fairly dense in habit, make excellent hosts for the early-flowering and double cultivars. The size of their flowers and the closeness of the blooms makes them very susceptible to wind damage, so, unless situated in a sheltered position, a shrub with an open framework of branches would not be a suitable host to these types. The wind could blow through, detaching the vines from the branches and causing considerable damage. There are, however, a wide range of more suitable varieties of shrubs from which to choose, including *Cotinus*, *Viburnum*, *Cotoneaster*, *Eleagnus*, *Escallonia* and shrub roses.

In addition to the colourful foliage that a range of these shrubs offer, many of them flower at the same time as clematis, providing opportunities for experimentation with contrasting flower shapes and colour associations. A possibility is the introduction of blue clematis into shrub roses, a colour which can range from the

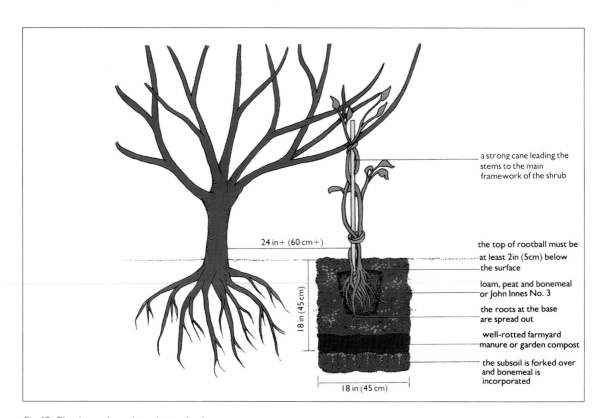

24 in+ (60 cm+)

18 in (45 cm)

18 in (45 cm)

a strong cane leading the stems to the main framework of the shrub

the top of rootball must be at least 2in (5cm) below the surface

loam, peat and bonemeal or John Innes No. 3

the roots at the base are spread out

well-rotted farmyard manure or garden compost

the subsoil is forked over and bonemeal is incorporated

Fig 49 Planting a clematis against a shrub.

Fig 50 'Gipsy Queen' climbing through a cotoneaster.

pale of 'Will Goodwin' to the much deeper 'Elsa Spath'. The white 'snowballs' of *Viburnum opulus* 'Sterile' make an incredible contrast to a good blue clematis such as 'Lasurstern', or the bright cerise-pink of 'Barbara Dibley'. The deep blue of one of the May and June flowering *Ceanothus*, such as *veitchianus*, would be complemented by the double flowers of the soft blue-mauve 'Vyvyan Pennell', or the dusky mauve pink of 'Proteus'.

Many shrubs have attractive foliage, ranging from light yellow-greens, which are good for displaying the bright pink and mauve clematis, through to the silvery-greys and rich purple-reds. Some, such as *Acer palmatum* 'Atropurpureum', with its brilliant purple foliage, are slow growing, but a mature specimen would make an excellent foil for the long, elegant pink sepals of

'John Warren', which, not being a vigorous plant, is unlikely to spoil the shape of the shrub. *Cotinus coggygria* 'Royal Purple' has a similar coloration to the acer and would provide a good background for some of the other pink clematis, such as the pearly-pink 'Dawn', that flowers so early in the season, 'Lincoln Star', with its raspberry-pink stripes, or the later delicate-looking flowers of 'Hagley Hybrid'. The season could be further extended by the *viticella* cultivars 'Little Nell' or 'Minuet', both of which have pale sepals edged with mauve. The purple-leaved shrubs also display pale blue clematis, such as 'H. F. Young,' 'Lady Caroline Nevill' or 'Perle d'Azur', to advantage. A stunning colour effect could be achieved by planting one of the new red varieties into a *Cotinus*. 'Allanah' is a very bright ruby-red with widely-spaced sepals and brown stamens, while 'Cardinal Wyszynski' is a brilliant crimson.

The white cultivars, together with the lavender-blue varieties such as 'Mrs Cholmondeley', combine well with silver and grey-leaved shrubs like *Elaeagnus commutata* and *Cytisus battandieri* to give a very cool impression. A lower-growing grey-leaved shrub is *Senecio greyi*. This makes an excellent host for *C. x durandii* or *C. eriostemon*. *C. x durandii* has stiff stems and unusual thick, ribbed, indigo-blue, bell-shaped flowers with distinctive cream stamens, while *C. eriostemon* has a profusion of smaller, deep violet-blue nodding flowers on much thinner stems. These varieties are semi-herbaceous, dying right back in the winter. As they have no twining leaf petioles, they have to be constantly tied up, unless they have the support of a low-growing shrub.

The *texensis* hybrids also require the support of shrubs as they too are unable to cling to their host. They have most unusual, pitcher-shaped flowers, which look rather like miniature tulips when they first come into bloom. 'Duchess of Albany' has deep pink flowers whilst 'Etoile Rose' is a deeper pink with silver margins. Another variety of the *texensis* type is 'Sir Trevor Lawrence', with its deep carmine,

Fig 51 C. integrifolia *'Durandii'*.

magnificent when grown over grey or silver foliage plants, as do 'Jackmanii', 'Gipsy Queen', or the dusky 'Mme Grange'. The inclusion of these late-flowering varieties extends the season of colour in the garden from May until September or October.

The imaginative gardener can find the possibilities of using clematis with trees and shrubs limitless. Almost all clematis could be used in conjunction with one shrub or another so that the list below is not comprehensive. It should be seen rather as a guide to varieties that would provide a good range of colour throughout the season, as well as being both robust in their habit of growth and floriferous.

Varieties for growing through shrubs and flowering in early summer include:

'Barbara Dibley'
'Barbara Jackman'
'Bee's Jubilee'
'Beauty of Worcester'
'Capitaine Thuilleaux'
'Miss Crawshay'
'Mrs Cholmondeley'
'Mrs George Jackman'
'Mrs Spencer Castle'
'Nelly Moser'
'Dr Ruppel'
'Elsa Spath'
'Fairy Queen'
'General Sikorski'
'Glynderek'
'H. F. Young'
'Joan Picton'
'Lasurstern'
'Lawsoniana'
'Lincoln Star'
'Lord Nevill'
'Marie Boisselot'
'Miss Bateman'
'Proteus'
'Richard Pennell'
'Ruby Glow'
'Saturn'
'Scartho Gem'

urn-shaped flowers. The rich ruby-red *C. texensis* 'Gravetye Beauty' is slightly different in that it opens out further into a star shape. These varieties are extremely robust when established, but they can be more difficult to get going than *durandii* or *eriostemon*. Slugs are very partial to the new shoots.

The *Artemisia abrotanum* (commonly known as 'Lad's Love'), together with *Senecio*', lends itself well to the draping qualities that the *viticella* and hard-pruning hybrid cultivars can take on when allowed to ramble amongst low-growing shrubs. In such situations, growing close to the ground, these tall varieties of clematis, which normally flower well above eye level, can be seen from such an angle that they take on quite a different appearance. The deep purple of *C. viticella* 'Royal Velours', or the slightly lighter colour of 'Etoile Violette', look

Fig 52 The flowers of C. texensis 'Gravetye Beauty' are almost tulip-like on first opening.

'Sealand Gem'
'Serenata'
'Sylvia Denny'
'The President'
'Wada's Primrose'
'W. E. Gladstone'

'Will Goodwin'
'William Kennett'

And for summer flowering all hard-pruning and *viticella* varieties would be suitable.

CHAPTER 7

Clematis as Ground Cover and Border Plants

The ability of clematis to grow horizontally as well as vertically is a characteristic of the species that is still under-exploited. They can be used either for ground cover, or in conjunction with other low-growing shrubs, perennials or even annuals. Additionally, there are clematis that are truly herbaceous, or can be grown as border plants, ranging from less than 3½ft (1m) to 7ft (2m) in height.

GROUND COVER

Clematis cannot be described as good ground cover plants in the accepted sense, as they are unlikely to be capable of smothering weeds, and they are mostly deciduous. The evergreen varieties of *C. cirrhosa*, which ramble about so charmingly in rocky outcrops in Mediterranean regions, are not ideally suited to growing in a similar situation in Britain because of possible frost damage. Clematis cannot take the place of other ground cover plants such as *Vinca* or *Lamium*, both of which have the ability to overcome all but the most tenacious of weeds, leaving a blanket of leaf that will cover the most difficult areas of the garden. If you expect your clematis to do this, you will be disappointed.

Clematis will most certainly not grow in the deep shade and dry soil to be found beneath trees. Neither will they survive in dank, wet corners of the garden. Whether they are to be grown vertically or horizontally, the require-ments for clematis are the same – they need good, moisture-retentive yet well-drained soil; some need full sunshine but others do better in partial shade. To some people, the term 'ground cover' is also synonymous with 'some-thing that will take care of itself'. However, the water requirements of clematis must be care-fully looked after, until the plant has become established with a root system that is deep enough to survive the vagaries of the British summer. It also follows that it is essential to remove all perennial weeds before planting, and that annual weeds should be kept down for the first year or two.

With their luxuriant habit of growth, and their ability to cover quite a large area in two or three years, the species varieties are perhaps the most suitable for growing in this context. In their natural surroundings, the alpinas, macro-petalas, and summer-flowering clematis such as *orientalis*, ramble at will. They scramble around rocky outcrops and clamber into low-growing trees and shrubs, making dense mounds of colour. It is in this type of uneven terrain that they are to be seen at their best. In the garden situation, a flat piece of ground can be altered by the strategic placing of some old branches off a hardwood tree.

Choice of Clematis

The type of clematis chosen to grow in a garden in this way will to some extent be determined by the sort of area to be covered,

Fig 53 C. montana *climbing over a rock garden in Japan.*

although more rampant varieties can be contained by pruning (*see* Chapter 3). Within three or four years tall-growing clematis, such as the *montana*, *vitalba* and *orientalis* types, could cover an area of up to about 10 x 10ft (3 x 3m), whilst the spring-flowering macropetalas and alpinas might cover about one-third of this space. However, with their natural habit of layering, these areas could be increased, over a period of time, to whatever is required.

Steep banks are frequently difficult to cultivate, but a clematis planted at the bottom and encouraged up the slope by the occasional pegging down of new shoots, will eventually make excellent coverage. The montanas or alpinas and macropetalas would be a good choice for this purpose, provided the bottom of the bank does not become waterlogged in the winter. In the first year fairly severe pruning is essential, to create a multi-stemmed plant

that will spread up the bank in several directions. The montanas can also be used for covering very large tree stumps, whilst the alpinas and macropetalas would be more suitable for the smaller ones. It is usually necessary to fasten a piece of chicken wire over the top of the stump, to provide an initial firm framework on to which the clematis can cling. The pink and white flowers of the montanas and the fragile-looking bells of the macropetalas and alpinas can completely transform an unsightly object in the spring. The leaves in summer, and the tracery of vines in the winter also create an acceptable coverage.

Immoveable rocks or boulders in the garden can provide an ideal setting for the yellow, lantern-shaped flowers and silky seed heads of *C. tangutica* and *C. orientalis*. The named varieties, such as *C. orientalis* 'Bill Mackenzie' or *C. orientalis* 'Burford Variety', are generally

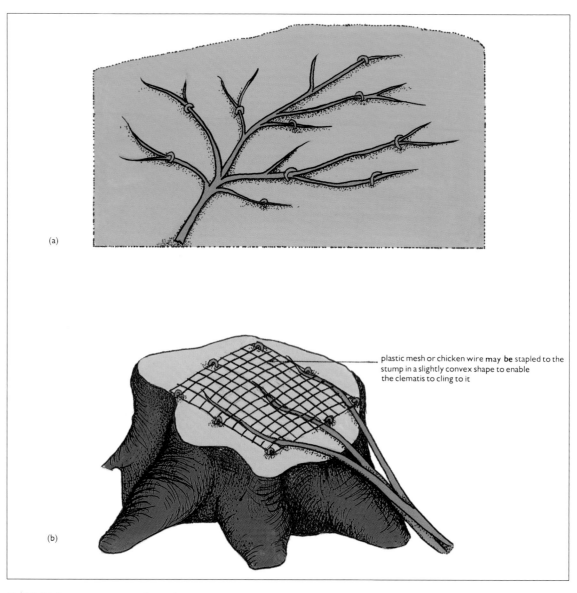

plastic mesh or chicken wire **may be** stapled to the stump in a slightly convex shape to enable the clematis to cling to it

(a)

(b)

Fig 54 *(a) A young* montana, *the main stems pegged down to create a framework of branches on a sloping bank. (b) A young* alpina *or* macropetala *planted against a tree stump. The support mesh will be quickly covered by a framework of stems.*

worthwhile growing, but many of the *orientalis* plants sold are grown from seed and will not necessarily have as good a flower as is possible. *C. glauca* is similar to *orientalis* but it has unusual greyish, glaucous, finely-cut leaves. *C. glauca var.* 'Akebioides' makes long, trailing silvery growths and has tiny yellow flowers with dark centres. One of the most attractive of these yellow-flowered clematis is *C. serratifolia*, a native of Korea, which has lemon-scented flowers followed by silky seed heads. All of these varieties grow well horizontally but, depending on their position in the garden, may need some pruning in February or March.

The clematis described above are all climbers, but there are two non-clinging varieties,

Fig 55 C. jouiniana *'Praecox' running through some rough ground. This is a non-climbing variety.*

C. jouiniana and *C. jouiniana* 'Præcox', which also make good ground cover plants. *C. jouiniana* is much sought after, but in many respects the variety 'Præcox' makes a much more satisfactory ground cover plant, as its leaves are larger and look very lush. It starts to flower in early August, being several weeks earlier than the type, which does not usually start to bloom until later in the month or early September. *C. jouiniana* has pale blue flowers, whilst 'Præcox' is pale mauve, fading down to almost white. They both bloom down the entire length of their trailing stems, the last flowers fading in October. A single plant will cover approximately 4 × 4ft (1·5 × 1·5m), and it is a variety that can be grown in very light woodland, provided the ground remains moist.

There are a number of other clematis species that are suitable for providing ground cover in expansive areas. These are included in the following list:

C. alpina and its cultivars
C. appifolia
C. connata
C. fargesii var. 'Soulei'
C. flammula
C. glauca
C. glauca var. 'Akebioides'
C. jouiniana
C. jouiniana 'Præcox'
C. macropetala and its cultivars
C. montana and related *montana* types
C. orientalis and its cultivars
C. rehderiana
C. serratifolia
C. tangutica
C. vitalba

HYBRID AND *VITICELLA* CULTIVARS

The hybrid and *viticella* cultivars are not ideal as ground cover plants in their own right, but they can be used to ramble over other low-growing plants and shrubs to advantage.

In the early part of this century, clematis were grown as bedding plants! Writing in 1935, Ernest Markham said 'the clematis also has definite claims to be considered as a bedding plant. At Gravetye we have planted beds of moderate size with selected varieties. For these we place in the beds, slantwise, small structures over which the growths ramble.' However delightful the structure may be when in flower, the prospect of the same in winter does not bear thinking about. Perhaps if the timbers were arranged in a cartwheel rather than random fashion, and if the varieties chosen were the late-summer-flowering ones that could be hard pruned and tidied up, the effect would be no worse than the average hybrid tea rose-bed in winter. The edges could even be softened by lavender or something similar. Certainly, clematis cultivars need to be raised off the ground to some extent, but a natural framework of living plants is surely preferable to hoisting them over dead branches. A garden or bed devoted entirely to clematis is not a good idea, as they are not the most attractive of plants in their winter state!

The Site

When selecting sites for prostrate-growing clematis, the criteria are similar to those which apply when planting into trees and taller shrubs. Consider how vigorous the clematis needs to be, and whether it is advantageous for it to be hard pruned. If the host plants flower, should the clematis bloom before, after, or at the same time? Would a large or small flower be appropriate, and should it be light or dark in tone? Another consideration is the maturity of the host plants. It is obviously desirable that host plants should be fairly well established,

otherwise the clematis will either choke them, or they will swamp the clematis. If this is not possible, their eventual size should be taken into account, spaces being filled with annual or other short-lived subjects.

It should also be remembered that in an established border, particularly if no real attention has been paid to the adding of nutrient in past years, the soil may well be exhausted and will not provide the conditions essential for a clematis to survive. It will be necessary to dig an adequate hole and add manure, and so on (*see* Chapter 2) and, as ever, pay careful attention to watering in the first season or two.

Choice of Clematis

The true herbaceous border has largely been replaced by a mixed border, including shrubs, herbaceous perennials, annuals, bulbs and sometimes climbing plants. Borders are frequently designed to have a peak season, when the impact of colour will be greatest. Clematis can be used either to enrich this display, or to provide colour over other plants when it is their 'off-peak' season. Borders designed for an optimum summer effect are often lacking in flower in May and June, but at that time the foliage of many summer-flowering shrubs looks superb and will provide a perfect foil for the early-flowering clematis. The fresh green of *Euonymus fortunei*, 'Emerald and Gold' would look wonderful with the clear pale blue of 'H. F. Young', or the deeper blue of 'Lasurstern'.

The leaves of *Hypericum* are plain green and essentially uninteresting, but, when grown in a partially shady situation, they provide a good background for the pink and white clematis. Of these, the first to come to mind would probably be 'Nelly Moser', which has proved so reliable over the years, but the list would also include 'Bee's Jubilee', 'Capitaine Thuilleaux' and 'Dr Ruppel', together with the somewhat less vigorous 'Lincoln Star' and 'John Warren', both of which have long pointed sepals. Two other compact-growing varieties, 'Carnaby' and

Fig 56 'John Warren', one of the many varieties raised by Walter Pennell.

'Asao,' are both deep pink, the former having a darker central bar.

Three very early-flowering varieties, all with well-rounded sepals and dark stamens, are 'Miss Bateman', which is white, 'Dawn', a very pale pink, and 'Lady Londesborough', which has a blue flower fading down to a pale silvery-grey. These all look well against a fairly dark green background, or the deep purple-red leaves of the dwarf *Berberis thunbergii* 'Atropupurea Nana', which in turn associates so well with grey and silver foliage plants such as lavenders or *Stachys lanata*.

The deep-coloured early-flowering hybrids, such as the deep violet 'Haku Ookan', 'Elsa Spath', 'Daniel Deronda' (semi-double), or 'Lord Nevill', whose deep blue flowers are held horizontally, are excellent against the silver-grey foliage of *Potentilla fruticosa* 'Manshu', which is a low-spreading variety with pure white flowers. The blue-green leaves of the prostrate junipers make an ideal setting for the brilliant violet-blue

and cerise colouring of 'Mrs N. Thompson', which, as it is not a vigorous grower, is well suited to meandering through other plants without becoming too invasive. In 1984, Jim Fisk introduced 'Wilhemina Tull', very similar in colour to 'Mrs N. Thompson' but a more robust performer. The prostrate cotoneasters also make excellent supports for clematis, but with the evergreen varieties it is perhaps better to limit your choice of clematis to the viticellas or late-summer-flowering varieties. It will be possible to cut away the old vines in the late autumn, and leave the glossy green foliage of *Cotoneaster dammeri* or *C. microphyllus* to brighten the garden in the depths of winter. Both the deep and pale colours of clematis can be delightful with many of the aromatic perennials and sub-shrubs, such as the silvery *Santolina* and *Artemesia* species, the glaucous grey-blue leaves of rue, and the silvery mauve of the purple-leaved sage.

The hard-pruning varieties, both hybrid and *viticella* cultivars, are well suited to hosts which themselves have to be cut back hard in the autumn or spring. The summer-flowering varieties can be chosen to bloom at the same time as many border plants, but tend to associate best with flowers of a similar colour range to their own, for example, the annual candytuft and asters, or the cranesbill geraniums. The deep purple and white varieties of clematis look wonderful trailing through campions (*Lychnis coronaria*), whose bright magenta flowers are held above woolly grey leaves. Grey or silver foliage is an invaluable backcloth for some of the stronger clematis colours. Although most clematis do not usually look well with large unrelieved blocks of yellow and orange, the blues of *C. x durandii* and *C. eriostemon* are quite vibrant when seen against the little yellow buttons of *Santolina* (cotton lavender) or the yellow daisies of *Senecio greyii*, which are softened by their skirts of grey leaves.

It is perhaps worth remembering at this point the value of clematis as a vertical feature within the border. The late-summer-flowering varieties are particularly useful to provide colour and height at a time when many of the early perennials have ceased to bloom. In addition to planting into shrubs, a pole or tripod can be used to give more height (*see* Chapter 9). The new growths should be tied in to their support as they grow, and within two or three seasons a variety such as 'Comtesse de Bouchaud' or 'Niobe' should completely clothe a pole in a column of bloom from late June onwards.

Heather Beds

In recent years the *viticella* cultivars seem to have taken on a quite specific ground cover role, now that the cult of the heather bed is upon us. With their dainty flowers, viticellas are used to enliven the winter-flowering ericas from July to October – the clematis being pruned back after flowering in November, in order that the full benefit of the heathers can be gained later. If they are not to be swamped, the heathers need to have been in place for at least a year before

Fig 57 C. viticella *'Margot Koster'*, one of the first viticellas to bloom in the summer.

clematis are introduced. In established heather beds, the occasional plant may need to be removed and the soil well prepared before the clematis is planted. To give good coverage the viticellas should be planted about 60in (150cm) apart.

When grown in juxtaposition like this, care should be taken with the tonal values of the clematis flowers when they are seen against the leaves of the heathers. Some of the viticellas are very dark in colour, and can only be displayed effectively against the light background of such golden-leaved ericas as *E. carnea* 'Aurea' and *E. carnea* 'Jack H. Brummage'. In this situation use *C. viticella* 'Etoile Violette', which has deep violet sepals, or *C. viticella* 'Royal Velours', which is the darkest of all, with lush, velvety purple flowers. Two red viticellas, the very showy *C. viticella* 'Kermasina', with its crimson sepals and a very dark eye, and the wine-red 'Mme Julia Correvon', also benefit from a light-coloured background. *Viticella* 'Abundance' shows well against the bright green leaves of many of the heathers, as does 'Margot Koster', both of which are pink. Two double viticellas in a similar colour range are the very old variety, 'Purpurea Plena Elegans', which is a mauve-pink, and the recently redis-covered and named 'Mary Rose', a little more spiky than the former and smoky-amethyst in colour. A fairly bright green or golden carpet of heathers is most suitable for the largest of the viticellas, 'Venosa Violacea'. Its boat-shaped sepals are 3in (7–8cm) across, and a rich violet broken with a network of white veining.

Paler Cultivars

The paler cultivars look well on either bright green or dark green foliage. Try *C. viticella* 'Little Nell', which has predominantly white sepals shading to pale mauve at the margins, or *C. viticella* 'Minuet', with its creamy-white central zone with purple-mauve veining, and a broad band of purple at the edge of the sepals. The flowers of *C. viticella* 'Alba Luxurians' are quite exquisite, with pure white sepals tipped with green and a contrasting dark eye, and are well worth considering in such a situation.

Naturally, the *viticella* cultivars can also be used to complement summer-flowering heathers and other herbaceous plants and shrubs. *C. x durandii* and *C. eriostemon*, together with the *texensis* hybrids (*see* Chapter 6), may also be used in a similar manner to the hybrid and *viticella* cultivars described above.

Varieties to ramble through a border

Light Pruning

'Alice Fisk'
'Asao'

'Barbara Dibley'
'John Warren'
'King George V'
'Lady Londesborough'
'Barbara Jackman'
'Bee's Jubilee'
'Bracebridge Star'
'Carnaby'
'Daniel Deronda'
'Dawn'
'Dr Ruppel'
'Duchess of Edinburgh'
'Elsa Spath'
'Hagley Hybrid'
'Haku Ookan'
'H. F. Young'
'Joan Picton'
'Lasurstern'
'Lincoln Star'
'Lord Nevill'
'Maureen'
'Miss Bateman'
'Mrs N. Thompson'
'Nelly Moser'
'Richard Pennell'
'Sir Garnet Wolseley'
'Snow Queen'
'The President'
'Violet Charm'
'Wada's Primrose'

Hard Pruning

'Allanah'
'Cardinal Wyszynski'
'Hagley Hybrid'
'Mme Edouard André'
'Niobe'
'Pink Fantasy'
'Prince Charles'
'Rouge Cardinal'
'Serenata'
'Twilight'
'Ville de Lyon'
'Voluceau'
'Warsaw Nike'

All other hard-pruning cultivars may be used but most grow taller than those listed.

C. eriostemon
C. x durandii
C. texensis 'Duchess of Albany'
C. texensis 'Etoile Rose'
C. texensis 'Sir Trevor Lawrence'
C. texensis 'Gravetye Beauty'
All C. viticella cultivars

HERBACEOUS AND SHRUBBY CLEMATIS

Most herbaceous varieties have flowers which are unlike those normally associated with clematis. They can be thick-sepalled bell shapes or tubular (the latter are often described as 'hyacinth-like' in catalogues). Some have extraordinarily large leaves, out of all proportion in size to their flower heads, and many are scented. Most of them are floppy plants which, unless they are going to be left to trail, require some form of support, either from other plants or by discreet staking with pea sticks, rather than being tied to individual canes. They behave like any other herbaceous plant in that they die back in winter. In February, they should be cut back to near the base of the plant, at which time they can, if necessary, be divided. All varieties can be propagated by division, and a few can be grown from seed. Quite a number of herbaceous clematis are worthy of a place in a fairly small border, if only for their scent. However, some are more suited to a large garden, and may perhaps be considered as 'collector's items' rather than for their value as garden plants.

Clematis integrifolia and its cultivars are some of the most effective border clematis. *C. integrifolia* is a European species growing to something less than 40in (100cm) in height. A mass of shoots develops from the crown each spring and each stem supports a thick-sepalled, bell-shaped flower which is a mid-indigo blue. It needs the support of sticks, unless the surrounding plants make this unnecessary. There are some good named cultivars on the market which are scented. The variety 'Olgae' has attractive pale blue sepals, whilst 'Rosea' is similar, with pink flowers, that are darker on the reverse. *C. integrifolia* 'Hendersonii' has slightly larger blue flowers which, like all the *integrifolia* cultivars, flowers from July to September.

Another sweetly-scented herbaceous clematis that makes a veritable thicket of new shoots from the crown each spring is *C. recta*. The individual creamy-white flowers are minute, but they are produced freely in large, loose panicles from June through to August. When it is established, it makes a large clump at least 40in (100cm) high and the same across. It will almost certainly need staking. The type has rounded, grey-green, glaucous leaves, whilst *C. recta* 'Purpurea' has bronzy-purple stems and foliage. *C. recta* can be grown from seed, but 'Purpurea' will not necessarily come true. Both can be propagated by division or cuttings.

Clematis heracleifolia is of a woody, shrubby habit with extremely large leaves and pale blue tubular or hyacinth-like flowers. There are a number of different cultivars which are all scented, but differently so. Perhaps the most striking and fragrant is *C. heracleifolia* 'Wyevale', growing to about 40in (100cm) in height and with very distinctive strong blue flowers. The varieties 'Campanile' and 'Davidiana' both have paler blue flowers and the typical coarse *heracleifolia* foliage. 'Mrs Robert Brydon' has much paler off-white flowers which have only a hint of blue. It can grow as high as 7ft (2m) and does need a strong support. The heracleifolias flower in August and September which makes them a useful contribution to the border.

There are other shrubby clematis bearing tubular flowers over coarse leaves, which are perhaps less useful in the small to medium-sized garden, but used in large clumps can make quite a feature in the right situation. *Clematis stans*, a native of Japan, is one of these. It grows to about

Fig 58 C. recta *'Purpurea'*, a scented variety with bronze-purple leaves.

60in (150cm) in height and has pale, off-white flowers. The two other semi-herbaceous, woody clematis, *C. jouiniana* and *C. jouiniana* 'Præcox', are more useful plants. As well as growing horizontally, they can be grown vertically if tied to a support, and can be seen fan-trained on to a wired wall. Grown in this way they can reach a height of 10ft (3m) or more. Another shrubby clematis that can attain a height of 7ft (2m) when planted against a wall is *C. songarica*, an autumn-flowering species from Siberia, with pure white starry clusters of flowers, and a hawthorn-like scent. *Clematis fusca*, from Manchuria, will grow to a similar height and has curious red-brown pitcher-shaped

flowers. It is another variety we would call a 'collector's item', and is a desirable plant for a large mixed border.

Good Scented Herbaceous Varieties

C. integrifolia 'Olgae'
C. integrifolia 'Rosea'
C. recta
C. recta 'Purpurea'
C. heracleifolia 'Campanile'
C. heracleifolia 'Davidiana'
C. heracleifolia 'Wyevale'
C. heracleifolia 'Mrs Robert Brydon'

CHAPTER 8

Clematis in Containers

'Can I grow a clematis in a tub?' is a question often asked of clematis suppliers. In theory, any clematis can be grown in a tub or container, with the same ground rules applying with regard to position as would apply to any other clematis in any other part of the garden. The only difference is that, particularly in the summer months, the owner takes over the responsibility for supplying the water, and it is this aspect of their care that basically determines which varieties are suitable for growing in containers and which are not.

CHOICE OF CLEMATIS

It is important for the propagator, if he is to be successful, to balance water availability against water loss (see Chapter 10). This is also the key to container culture, and will determine which varieties of clematis are most suitable for growing in this way. Compare a mature *montana* with an equally well-established 'Hagley Hybrid'. The former will grow to a height of 35ft (10m) or more, will cover vast areas of building, and will give a display of spring flowers that could hardly be described as modest. The 'Hagley Hybrid', by contrast, remains short in stature, relatively compact and with an intense show of flower which is relative to its size. Both plants will be losing water throughout the spring and summer by transpiration through the leaves. The *montana*, with many times the number of leaves, will be using far more water and will develop a much larger root system through which these needs can be supplied. For this reason a container the size of a bath tub

would probably not be large enough to sustain a plant that was big enough to cover a garage, while the owner, during a hot spell in the summer, might well have to water two or three times a day to meet the plant's needs – the smaller the tub, the less the water reserve, and the greater the number of times it will need watering. At the same time, if the container is badly drained or standing in a reservoir of water, there is always the risk of the bottom of the tub becoming waterlogged and the roots rotting.

The 'Hagley Hybrid', with its modest growth, lower water requirements and smaller root system, would be a much more suitable variety to grow in this way; even here a container measuring about 18in (45cm) across and deep is recommended – one of the half-barrels often seen on sale in garden centres is ideal. Although the root system of a small variety like this may not fill such a container, the size is useful in that the additional compost will act as a reservoir and reduce the frequency of watering. It is impossible to say how much water a mature plant growing in such a tub will need, so much depends on recent rainfall, temperature, humidity and the size of the plant, and this is where the observant eye of the owner is crucial. He will have to assess his plant's needs by observation, and in a hot spell a mature plant could require a good soaking with two or three gallons (9–14 litres) of water perhaps once to three times a week. If there is a significant amount of rain, if the weather becomes cooler or if the plant begins to die back for the winter, little or no added water will be necessary for the clematis.

Fig 59 The high density of housing in Japan forces many clematis lovers to grow their plants in containers. This is 'H. F. Young'.

TRAINING

There are many people who grow their plants in containers from choice, and use them as free-standing features in courtyards, on patios, and so on. Provided he has the time, the gardener may train the vines of his clematis. This can be done to create a tight spiral, so that the total height of the plant is only about 4ft 6in (1·5m) above the compost and only a 12in (30cm) pot is needed. Great care is needed to train the vines in this fashion without breaking them, and the practice is really only ideal for those who do not have a vast expanse of general garden to attend. Still, the rewards can be great. The Japanese, who grow very many clematis in this fashion, write of 150 blooms or more on plants that are only about 60in (150cm) in height.

COMPOST

Clematis grown in tubs are going to require a rich compost in which to grow. John Innes No. 3, to which some peat and, if available, leaf mould have been added, is ideal. If the container is particularly large, some good garden soil could be added to this as an economy measure, but such soil must be open enough to allow good drainage. As it becomes exhausted, the compost will need topping up or partially replacing from time to time. Some growers re-pot annually, to ensure that the richness of the growing medium is maintained throughout the pot. To assist drainage, crocks should be placed in the bottom of the tub before filling, whilst the tub itself should be slightly raised off any surface on which it stands; pieces of broken quarry tiles would give sufficient height for this. During the growing season, weak liquid fertiliser can be added, up to two or three times a week. Tomato fertiliser, high in potash, seems very suited to this.

TYPES OF CONTAINERS

Half-barrels and purpose-made wooden containers of similar construction have the advantage of being strong, comparatively light for their size, and good thermal insulators. The roots of plants grown in them are protected from extremes of temperature, not as well as in the ground itself, but far better than would be the case with many of the alternatives. Wood is a material that can breathe, and the very method of construction will usually allow some air to get through to the compost to help keep it fresh and active. One disadvantage of wood is that periodically it will need to be emptied and the timber treated with a wood preservative. The frequency with which this needs to be done will vary, depending on the type of wood used in manufacture, and what treatment it was given at the time. Any of the recognised wood preservatives will do for this,

Fig 60 'Miss Bateman', which can be one of the first of the large-flowered varieties to bloom in the spring.

provided the manufacturers state that it may be used near plants. In any case it is advisable to wait until most of the smell has evaporated before using the container again. *Do not use creosote*. The fumes are long lasting and will damage, if not kill, your plant.

There are many plastic containers on the market that are sold for use in this sort of situation. These cannot be recommended for anything other than short-term use. The plastic soon becomes brittle, it will break very easily in cold weather, and it is a good thermal conductor, so the roots of your plants will over-heat in the summer and get far too cold in the winter. Many such containers will also distort under the weight of the plant, particularly in warm weather when the plastic can become less rigid.

Terracotta pots are quite good as, being porous, they allow air to pass through to the compost. They also drain well, and are good insulators from extremes of heat. There are two basic types on the market – those that are cast and those that are thrown. The thrown ware is much stronger than cast ware, which can crack very easily and must be stored inside during the winter. It is usually quite easy to see which method has been used to make the pot – on a hand-thrown pot, the ridges left by the potter's hands can be felt and often seen in the pot wall, while with a cast pot there is usually a vertical line to be seen on the pot wall where the two parts of the mould have joined.

Concrete containers are available, but they tend to be very heavy for their size and, being non-porous, can be cold in winter, while getting very hot in the summer. However, they are much better than plastic.

The use of what might be described as

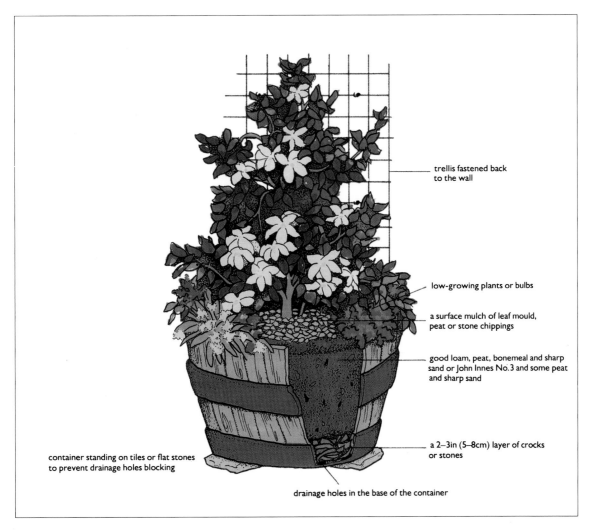

trellis fastened back
to the wall

low-growing plants or bulbs

a surface mulch of leaf mould,
peat or stone chippings

good loam, peat, bonemeal and sharp
sand or John Innes No.3 and some peat
and sharp sand

a 2–3in (5–8cm) layer of crocks
or stones

container standing on tiles or flat stones
to prevent drainage holes blocking

drainage holes in the base of the container

*Fig 61 A large container may be planted with low-growing subjects as well
as the clematis. Good drainage is essential.*

'found containers' can be exciting and interesting, inappropriate and ugly, or, in some cases, disastrous – so much depends on the nature of the container, where it is used and what it might have previously contained. Old troughs, sinks, and Victorian chimney pots can all do a superb job in the right setting, or look bizarre when used without sensitivity. Any receptacle that could have contained any form of chemical must be thoroughly cleaned before use – some chemicals are very persistent and could harm your plants. Care must also be taken to ensure adequate drainage. Rotten and hollowed-out

tree stumps are not really suitable for clematis as they can become too wet and encourage disease in your plant.

Purpose-built planters, although not moveable like most containers, are often constructed for growing clematis. The same guidelines concerning size and depth apply to these as to any other type of tub – they should be a minimum of a 20in (50cm) cube. These are usually made of bricks or stone, and should have good drainage holes at the base which are large enough not to become easily blocked. If the planter is built on to a concrete path such holes

83

are essential, but it is a good idea to include them even when building over a bed of soil to prevent waterlogging in the winter.

TUBS IN WINTER

The great advantage of growing clematis in tubs is that they can be moved into sheltered positions for the winter, thereby protecting the plants from the worst of the weather. In Norway, where the flowers of the early-summer-flowering varieties are usually lost because of the harshness of the winter, people often grow their clematis in containers – these are stored in cellars over the winter period to ensure a good display of flower the following year. Of course, there is the added advantage of being able to have different varieties in new positions for each season. The amount of protection required by clematis growing in containers will vary very much, according to the thickness and thermal qualities of that container and its position in the garden. Clematis do mind their roots being frozen, and will be damaged by the repeated thawing and freezing that occurs if a plant is in a thin-walled container in an exposed position. In a normal winter there will be times when the whole pot will freeze solid every night, only to thaw completely in the sun the next day. Such plants should be re-potted into more suitable containers or moved. Failing either of these alternatives, tie thick bundles of straw round the pot and lower parts of the plant in the late autumn and cover with a polythene sheet to keep out the rain. Wet straw will offer little or no protection.

Fig 62 Spiral form of training to produce a compact plant.

SUPPORTS FOR CLEMATIS IN TUBS

Where a clematis is grown in a container to climb up a wall or into a shrub in the normal way, the types of support detailed (see pages 86–91) will be quite adequate. When the clematis is planted in a pot to become a free-standing object, perhaps to be moved in the winter, other methods need to be used. Such plants will usually need far more attention and will need tying into their support very frequently, perhaps twice a week in early summer. Most people will probably work on a series of vertical sticks or canes, to which hoops or wires are attached every so often up the height. The object here will be to construct a framework up which the clematis can climb, and which it will eventually completely clothe on coming into flower. The gardener will have to relate the size of structure to the growing potential of the plant and choose materials which will merge into the plant itself if it is not completely covered. The final effect would be of a clematis 'bush'.

VARIETIES SUITABLE FOR GROWING IN A CONTAINER

Spring-Flowering

All alpinas and macropetalas

Early-Summer-Flowering

All the May/June large-flowered hybrids, including the double varieties, can be grown in a container, but the small number listed are particularly well suited by virtue of their compact habit of growth.

'Alice Fisk'
'Asao'
'Carnaby'
'Corona'
'Dawn'
'Haku Ookan'
'Joan Picton'

'H. F. Young'
'Lady Londesborough'
'Miss Bateman'
'Mrs N. Thompson'
'Sir Garnet Wolseley'

Midsummer-Flowering

'Elsa Spath'
'John Warren'
'Maureen'
'Snow Queen'
'The President'

Late-Summer-Flowering

Many of the late-summer-flowering varieties are rather tall, making them less suitable for container growing than the shorter varieties listed below.

'Allanah'
'Cardinal Wyszynski'
'Comtesse de Bouchaud'
'Hagley Hybrid'
'John Huxtable'
'Mme Edouard André'
'Niobe'
'Pink Fantasy'
'Prince Charles'
'Rouge Cardinal'
'Twilight'
C. viticella 'Mme Julia Correvon'

CHAPTER 9

Artificial Supports

There are many natural hosts through and over which a clematis will climb and scramble. However, because of the nature of both houses and gardens, it is usually necessary to give the clematis some aid in their search for greater height by building supports and structures especially for them. It is outside the scope of this book to give designs and plans for suitable structures which, in any case, usually need to be designed for a particular spot to be successful. However, it is hoped that the guidelines included will enable the gardener to support his plants in as personal a way as possible.

TRELLIS

It must be remembered with this, or any other type of support, that most clematis climb by means of twisting leaf petioles; that is, the stem of the leaf will grow round any convenient object as an anchor for its further growth. To do this, there must be room for the leaf to grow right round its support, if that support is to be of any use. Trellis is often seen nailed firmly back against a bare wall. Unless the wall is very uneven, this method of fixing makes it difficult for the clematis to become sufficiently attached to withstand the rigours of a good gale. When attached to a flat surface, trellis should always be fixed with spacers or laths behind it, say ¾in (18mm) thick. These laths should first be treated with wood preservative (*not* creosote — the fumes from it could kill your clematis). Slater's laths, obtained from builders' merchants, are quite good for this job, as they are usually sold ready treated. It is

important that the laths are securely fixed before the trellis is attached. On brickwork it is usually best to attach it by using plugs and screws, putting these fixings into the bricks themselves if the mortar is at all weak.

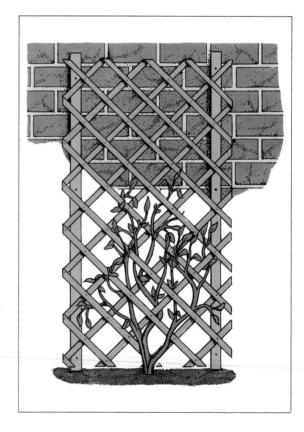

Fig 63 Wooden trellis fixed to the wall by means of vertical laths of wood. This allows space between the trellis and the wall to enable the stems and petioles to twine right round the support.

HORIZONTAL WIRES

These are probably the least noticeable of artificial supports. They do require a little more of the gardener, since he will have to go round his clematis regularly to tie them in, particularly when they are growing fast or when high winds are forecast. Galvanised or plastic-covered wire 2mm thick (14 standard wire gauge), fixed horizontally against a wall or fence from about 24in (60cm) upwards at 6–9in (15–22cm) is sufficient. There are a variety of ways in which these can be fixed:

1. Vertical battens fixed to the wall at about 6ft (2m) intervals, to which the wires are fixed with fencing staples.
2. Galvanised 'vine eyes', which are obtainable either to be hammered into the mortar courses of a wall, or with threads to be screwed into wall plugs or wood. Wires are passed through the ends of these and pulled tight.
3. Galvanised screw eyes, obtainable from a good ironmonger and used as above.

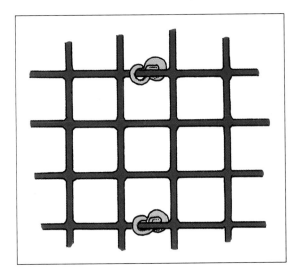

Fig 64 To facilitate maintenance on a rendered or painted surface, plastic-coated clematis trellis can be attached to the wall by means of large hooks, enabling the whole thing to be lifted down.

With all these methods, the wire needs to be pulled really tight; slack wires not only look unsightly, but also may not give a firm enough support to clematis stems to prevent damage. If you have a large amount of wire to tighten it is probably best to borrow a wire strainer from a tool hire firm for a day. This should not cost very much. With only a small quantity to do, a mole wrench and a bit of ingenuity will normally make a worthwhile job. Wire can also be used between vertical posts, as with a wire fence; such posts should not be placed much more than 6ft (2m) apart.

POSTS

Single posts placed in a border or beside paths can provide additional ways of supporting clematis when wall or other space is becoming short, or if a plant is required as a focal point in the garden. When established, a clematis grown in this way can, depending on variety, become large and bushy, offering a reasonable area of resistance to any wind. It is necessary, therefore, to think in terms of posts 10–12ft (3–4m) long as a minimum, and with a diameter at the base of about 6in (15cm). If these are erected with 30–40in (75–100cm) in the ground, to give adequate support when windy, you are still only left with about 9ft (3m) of height up which the clematis can climb, and many are capable of greatly exceeding this. As clematis do not climb in a corkscrew fashion like a runner bean, wires will need to be attached to the post to which the plant can cling. Such wires will need to be held away from the surface of the pole, if the clematis is going to be able to obtain adequate support. This space can be obtained by passing the wire over small blocks nailed at the top and bottom of the post, or by using longer lengths of wood and attaching the wires to their ends. A third method is to drive wooden pegs into the soil 3–6ft (1–2m) from the base of the post. Wires attached to the top of the post are taken down and attached to these pegs, giving a

87

Fig 65 A Japanese bamboo fence supports 'The President'.

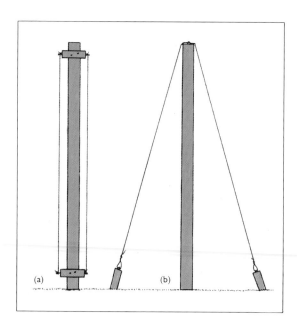

Fig 66 (a) Wires attached to small blocks of wood nailed to the top and bottom of the post. (b) Wires stapled to the top of the post are taken down and attached to pegs driven into the ground, giving a triangular structure.

triangular structure. This gives the plant more room to grow sideways, as well as giving some extra support to the post. When using any of these methods, attach the wires to the top of the post before it is put in place; attaching them later is not easy! Plant the clematis a little distance away from the post base, as this will facilitate replacing the post should this become necessary in the more distant future.

PERGOLAS, COLONNADES AND OTHER SUPPORTING STRUCTURES

These can be interesting to plan and build, and quite a focus of attention when finished and covered in clematis blossom. Reference to old catalogues or the illustrations in books on garden history, which are a rich source of inspiration, will often spark off ideas which can be converted into structures, and can provide novel solutions to the problem of supporting

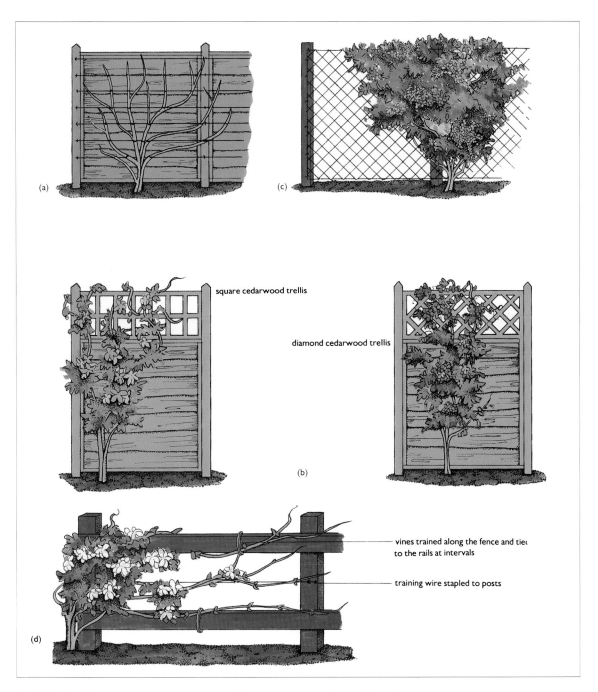

square cedarwood trellis

diamond cedarwood trellis

vines trained along the fence and tied to the rails at intervals

training wire stapled to posts

(a)

(b)

(c)

(d)

Fig 67 (a) Training wires are necessary for larch lap, or interwoven fences. The wires should be held away from the fence panels to allow the clematis to twine around them. (b) The maximum height for most fencing panels is 6ft (2m). There are many clematis in the 6–9ft (2–3m) range which are suitable, and extra height can be achieved by using longer posts and a trellis extension. (c) An unsightly chain link fence can be totally obscured by a montana or other vigorous species variety. (d) The flowers of some varieties, such as 'Marie Boisselot' and 'Lord Nevill', are held horizontally. They are ideally suited to being trained along a low fence where they can be viewed from above.

Fig 68 C. orientalis 'Sherriffii', a variety that can grow well when supported by a post.

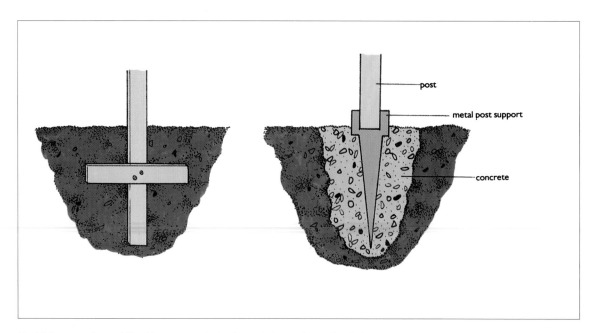

post

metal post support

concrete

Fig 69 Posts can be stabilised by means of a horizontal piece of wood nailed on below ground level, or, if more strength is required, metal post supports can be purchased.

Fig 70 Clematis macropetala *'Anders', recently introduced from Sweden.*

clematis and other climbers in the garden. Severe storms can wreak havoc with such structures, even when they are properly erected, and a moderate gale can be equally disastrous, where the structure is poorly built. The need to build well should be at the forefront of the gardener's mind when he starts to plan what is needed. That which would survive all aspects of the weather for many years as an open, un-clothed, construction, might fail very quickly when carrying both the weight and wind resistance of a vigorous *montana*.

Wood, treated or otherwise, erected straight into the soil has a limited life, according to soil conditions, and the type of timber used.

A useful range of metal fencing post sockets is now on the market and if these are used to support the main timbers of any wood structure, they will greatly lengthen its life and facilitate replacement in the future. The extra expense is well worth while in places where there are strong winds. In exposed areas the sockets are best cemented into the ground.

It is advisable when planning any form of garden structure to think ahead to future maintenance. With a little forethought, plants can be detached with the minimum of disturbance to allow areas to be repaired or retreated with wood preservative, provided this is considered in the initial construction.

CHAPTER 10

Propagation

The best way to succeed as a propagator is to fail, failure being the best teacher. This apparent contradiction makes more sense when the implications are further considered. If you are lucky and succeed in rooting cuttings at your first attempt (and it is cuttings that are being considered here), you will not necessarily be able to repeat that success a second time, and you may have learned very little in the process. However, by failing, or by only having partial success, you are made to consider what you have done and where you are going wrong. Successful propagating cannot be learned from a book; a book can only outline a way of working and point you in the right direction. Real success can only come from first-hand experience and your own observations.

In comparison with other varieties of plant, clematis are not easy to propagate *en masse*, and even in large nurseries the failure rate can be quite high with some varieties. If all that is required are one or two extra plants, this can be quite easy, but for any more, time, patience and determination are essential. There are four main ways of propagating clematis: layering, growing from seed, cutting, and division. (There is a fifth method – grafting – but this is less often practised and is highly skilled, so is outside the scope of this book.)

LAYERING

Consider our wild friend, the native *C. vitalba* or 'Old Man's Beard', and look at how it establishes itself in the hedgerow. This is an easy and reliable method of reproducing the cultivars in your garden. An established *vitalba* will show that the vines from the initial plant (and it is often difficult to distinguish which this is) have some-times had no real support from the hedge, or have been blown out of it. Where they have touched the ground, roots have formed, making a new plant which, if severed from the parent, will continue to thrive and show all the same characteristics. Over a period of many years, the wild *vitalba* can move many yards down the hedgerow, leapfrogging its way until eventually a *vitalba* hedge is created. This is the process of 'layering'. It is not as successful with all cultivars as it is with *vitalba*, but it does provide an easy way to produce extra plants. This is a traditional method, not favoured much by nurserymen for clematis as it is too slow to meet the public demand for plants.

The process of layering is quite straight-forward. A strongly-growing vine of clematis is carefully bent down until part of it touches the soil. The bend should not be sharp, as it is important not to crack or break a vine. Choose a leaf node which will easily touch the soil without putting too much strain on the stem. With a sharp knife carefully cut under the stem a sliver of wood, about 1 in (2–3cm) long, slightly deeper than the bark, cutting towards the node. Intro-duce some rooting compound on to the surface of the cut and bury the whole node about 1 in (2–3cm) deep in the surrounding soil. Pin down with two U-shaped pieces of wire, one on each side of the node and, to ensure that it is completely firm and will not move in a gale, add a large stone or brick. As an alternative, the node can be buried in a 4in (10cm) flower pot filled with lightly firmed-down John Innes Compost No. 2,

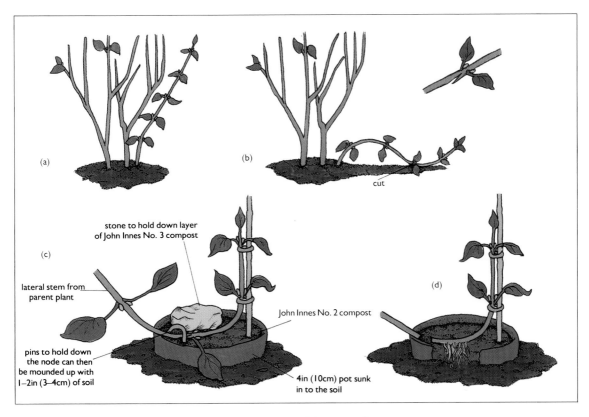

stone to hold down layer
of John Innes No. 3 compost

(a)

(b)

cut

(c)

lateral stem from
parent plant

pins to hold down
the node can then
be mounded up with
1–2in (3–4cm) of soil

John Innes No. 2 compost

(d)

4in (10cm) pot sunk
in to the soil

Fig 71 Layering. (a) Choose a suitable stem that will easily bend down to soil level. (b) Make an angled cut 1in (2·5cm) into the node. (c) Peg the layer down firmly into compost and tie the shoot to a bamboo cane. (d) Eventually, sever the rooted layer from the parent plant.

and the pot buried in the ground in a suitable position. Using the pot avoids any disturbance of the roots when the new plant is eventually separated from its parent in about a year's time. Support the shoot with a stake, and make sure that both the parent plant and the pot do not dry out while rooting is taking place.

Mature, hardwood layers are best started in the late autumn and left in place for a year to eighteen months. Newer but not 'green' wood layers may be started in the late spring or summer, but they should be left in place until the autumn of the following year. It is wise to treat a few vines in this way at the same time as they might not all take.

PROPAGATION FROM SEED

Clematis are often valued as much for their marvellous seed heads as for the flowers which precede them. Many gardeners have gathered these, thinking this to be the easiest method of propagation. With some varieties this is so, but with many it is not to be recommended. To understand why, it is necessary to appreciate the difference between hybrid and species varieties. The species varieties are those which are the wild flowers of other countries, in the same way that *vitalba* is a wild flower in northern Europe – *C. flammula* can be found growing in the hedgerows of Provence, *C. viticella* in Spain, and so on. These will normally

93

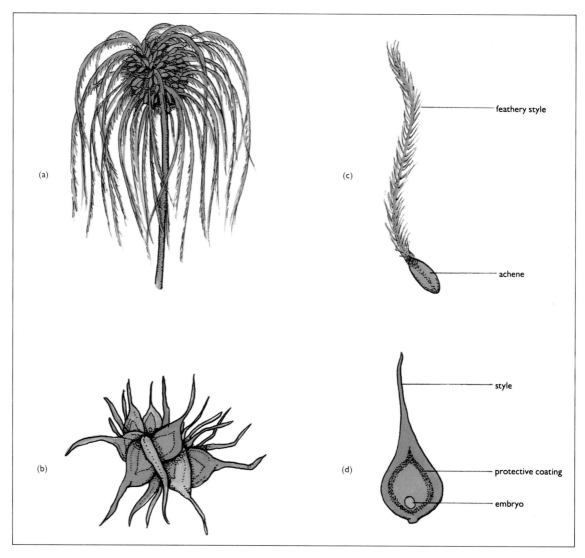

Fig 72 (a) Clematis orientalis *seed head. (b) Seed head from a hybrid cultivar.*
(c) This achene has only a thin protective coating and will germinate
quickly. (d) This achene has a thicker coating, and will therefore take longer
to germinate.

grow true from seed, but, as with weeds in the garden, there are good and bad specimens and all will not grow with the same size and vigour, or have the same size of flower as the parent. There is many a *montana* to be seen in the spring, which may well have originated from indifferent seedlings, and grow with all the energy of the variety but have a comparatively poor flower.

Hybrids, and this includes all the large-flowered varieties, will not generally come true from seed, and seed is not a good vehicle for

Fig 73 'Lincoln Star', best planted out of full sun to prevent fading.

reproducing a favourite specimen in the garden. The hybrids are usually the result of a deliberate cross between two other varieties, this crossing taking place at the flowering stage. The seeds from this cross are collected and sown and, when they eventually flower three or four years later, each seed will produce a plant that will show some of the characteristics of each parent, but none will be identical to them. Many well-known clematis varieties have come about by chance rather than through the deliberate crossing of two varieties. The flowers of 'Bracebridge Star' and 'Lincoln Star' resulted from the random collection of the seed heads of 'Nelly Moser' by Walter Pennell. Out of fifty or so plants grown in this way from one seed head, the nurseryman may find one or two that are sufficiently good and different from known varieties to be produced commercially. Sometimes these chance seedlings can give the grower a surprise – 'Edith', a white variety, was produced from a seed from 'Mrs Cholmondeley'. However, the hybridiser can deliberately cross two varieties where he feels there is a chance that the qualities of two different blooms, if combined into one plant, could produce a new worthwhile variety.

Although propagation from seed is unreliable, it may be interesting to plant collected seeds just to see what sort of flower is produced – you may be lucky and produce a new variety of your own (all new hybrids start from seed). You can be sure of one thing, each of the plants will be unique. However, any new variety produced in this way would need to be significantly different from anything else that was already on the market for a nursery to be interested enough to take it further.

Seed Collection and Storage

The clematis seed head is comprised of many individual achenes or fruiting bodies, each with a feathery tail. There are considerable differences in their size and appearance, with many being extremely decorative. Some of the early and mid-season hybrid cultivars produce a rigid structure, almost like a cage protecting the seeds within. The *orientalis* types have long silky tails, whilst those of some of the species varieties, like *C. recta*, have spiky seed heads. The size of the actual seed, or achene, can vary considerably, as can the thickness of the protective coating: the thicker the seed coating, the slower the germination. Small seeds like those of *C. tangutica* can germinate in ten to fourteen days, given ideal conditions, but the larger seeds of the hybrids can take six months, a year, or even longer.

Seed heads ripen at different times according to their flowering season. In a good hot summer the seed from 'Nelly Moser' will be ripe in September or October, whilst at that time, the seed heads of *C. flammula* would, in the UK, only just be forming. The green seeds or achenes gradually turn brown as they ripen, their tails becoming lighter in colour and more fluffy. When completely ripe, they can be removed from the old flower stalk with ease.

Ideally, seed should be collected from the plant when it has fully ripened on the vine, but this is not always possible as seed heads have to be gathered at any opportune moment. This raises the problem of drying and storage. Obviously, if a seed head has been collected whilst it is still underripe, it will have to be allowed to dry out and fully ripen. This can best be done by leaving it in a cool, dry, airy place. Unless it is undergoing a process of stratification, which is not usually necessary for clematis, the seed should not be stored damp as it can be subject to mould. Neither should it be dried excessively, as a certain amount of moisture is necessary within the seed, to liberate the energy and initiate growth when conditions become favourable. Given the opportunity, seed is best collected on a dry day but if, as so often happens, it has to be collected when the atmosphere is damp, the seed should be spread out to dry for a few hours on a sheet of paper indoors before it is labelled and packed. Seed is best stored sealed in a polythene bag placed in a domestic refrigerator. Like this it should remain viable for twelve months stored at a temperature of 35°F (2–3°C). Seed should not be placed in a freezer.

Time of Sowing

The seeds of the early-flowering cultivars like 'Nelly Moser' can be sown as soon as they have ripened in September or October. However, there seems little advantage in this compared to spring sowing in March, as seeds do not start into growth until conditions are right. The first warm day in spring is not sufficient to activate the tiny embryos into growth, for they must have sustained warmth before they begin to develop.

In their natural environment, a considerable percentage of seed heads remain on the vine until the spring; many of those falling to the ground before this may well have rotted or have been eaten. When the time is right the individual achenes break away from the old flower stalk, fall to the ground, and eventually germinate as the soil warms up and the day length increases. This natural sequence of events is worth noting – to activate the seeds of a fast-germinating variety into growth too early spells disaster for the vulnerable emerging seedlings, unless ideal frost-free conditions can be guaranteed.

Method of Sowing

For germination to take place seeds need adequate supplies of warmth, moisture and air. The temperature at which trays of seedlings are kept is not critical, but germination will be quicker if some heat is available, ideally 59–64°F (15–18°C). Fill seed trays to a good depth with proprietary seed compost. This depth of

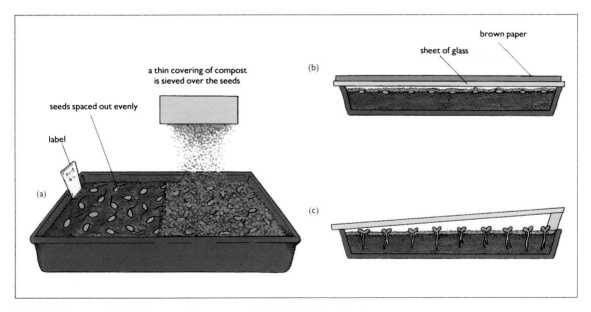

Fig 74 Sowing seed. (a) Fill the tray with compost which is lightly firmed and then soaked before sowing. (b) After watering with a fine rose, cover the seed tray with a sheet of glass, then a sheet of brown paper. For seeds which will take longer to germinate, a piece of slate or tile is more appropriate. Do not allow surface compost to dry out. (c) Remove the brown paper as soon as the seeds germinate. Increase the ventilation by propping up the glass, and shade from bright sunlight.

97

compost is important, as clematis seedlings quickly develop long roots. The type of compost does not seem to be too important, provided that it is moisture-retentive and of a fairly open texture to facilitate the removal of the seedlings without damage to the roots. Nutrient in the compost is unnecessary as each seed contains within itself enough food to sustain its initial growth.

Space the seeds out evenly on the compost (which has been gently firmed down in the seed trays). Cover them only to their own depth with compost or they will fail to germinate. The inclusion of grit in the covering compost alters the colour, therefore making it possible to see that the seeds are not being covered too thickly.

After sowing, water the compost, and then, to conserve moisture, cover the seed tray with glass followed by brown paper, or an old compost bag. If the seed is of a hybrid variety which will take a long time to germinate, a slate or tile is more satisfactory than glass and brown paper. The compost must not be allowed to dry out, so inspect trays regularly and water as necessary. These trays are best placed in a greenhouse or cold frame. When germination has taken place the covers should gradually be removed, giving more light and ventilation. As the seedlings grow, they will need maximum light but do not place them in a position where they can be scorched by the sun.

As soon as the seedlings are large enough to handle, which is usually when the first pair of

Fig 75   Jim Fisk's cross between 'Lasurstern' and 'Mrs Cholmondeley', 'Alice Fisk'.

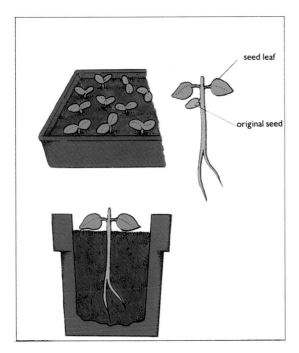

seed leaf

original seed

Fig 76 Planting seedlings. (a) When the seedlings are ready to be pricked out, they must be handled only by the leaves. (b) Plant the seedlings with the seed leaves only just above the surface of the compost. After watering, the pot should be kept closed for a few days with a propagator top or polythene bag. Ventilation is gradually increased, and then the top is finally removed.

leaves has fully expanded, they can be pricked out in the usual manner. Use small thumb pots or plastic multi-packs filled with a good potting compost. Return the seedlings to the glasshouse or frame to be kept close for a few days until they get over the shock of transplanting. Ventilation can then be gradually increased. Pot on the young plants when they are large enough, usually the following autumn, and then, some twelve months after germination, the young clematis can be planted out in their permanent positions in the garden or grown on in larger pots.

HYBRIDISATION

Although this does not strictly come under the heading of propagation, it is convenient to cover it here where easy reference can be made to the section on seeds. The actual process of hybridisation is straightforward, but does require some delicate work with a sharp knife. Some deliberate cross-fertilisation can take place by collecting the pollen from one flower with a small soft paintbrush and introducing this to the stigma of the recipient flower, but such a method is haphazard and there is no certainty that only the pollen from the one variety will fertilise the recipient plant. A more methodical way of working is required to do the job properly, without the risk of stray pollination from another source.

Having chosen the two varieties to be crossed, a good bud should be selected on one, just at the point when it is about to open. Taking care not to bend and damage the stem, carefully go round the bud and cut off all the sepals. Sometimes this can be done with a small pair of sharp scissors, but it is often easier to use a small pointed craft knife with a new blade, particularly if you are working on the bud of a double variety. To avoid this flower pollinating itself, the anthers must also be removed. This is achieved by cutting through the filaments which support them. All that will be left now is the pistil supporting the stigma, surrounded by a 'skirt' composed of the stubs of the stamens and sepals. This is the part of the flower you need to pollinate. At this stage it is not ready, and it must be left for two or three days until the stigma becomes sticky and excretes a viscous liquid. During this time, cover it with a polythene bag tied to the stem with a twist tie, to prevent any 'foreign' pollen reaching the stigma. When it is adjudged to be in a suitable state, pick a recently-opened flower off the other variety to be used and, with a clean watercolour brush, collect the pollen from the flower and apply to the stigma of the first flower. If possible, this should be done when it

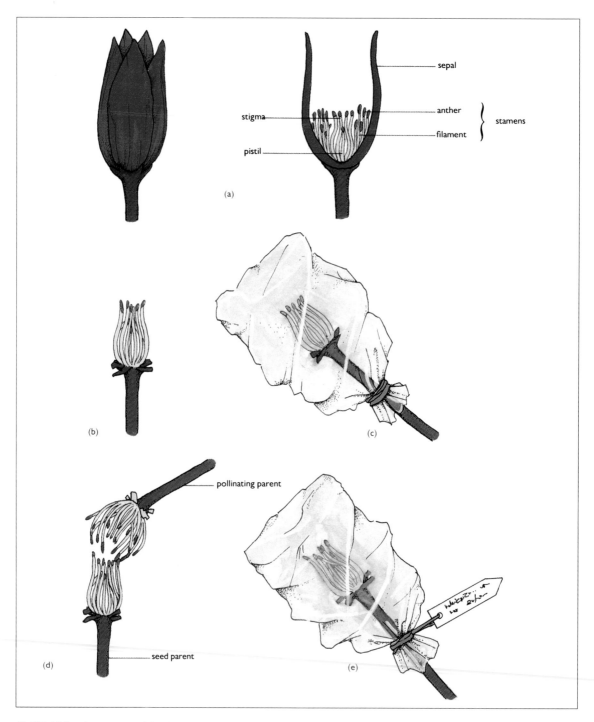

Fig 77 (a) Seed parent sepals just beginning to open. The flower has not yet been pollinated by insects. (b) The sepals and stamens have been removed, leaving only the stigma. (c) The stigma enclosed in a polythene bag to prevent it being pollinated. (d) Pollen is either brushed on to the stigma with an artist's paintbrush, or transferred directly from the anthers of the pollinating parent. (e) Replace the polythene bag and leave for a week or two, then remove and leave the seed head on the plant to ripen. Label clearly, naming the seed parent first.

is warm and sunny. The pollinated stigma is then re-covered with the polythene bag, taking care the stigma does not touch the polythene itself. Tie the polythene to the stem loosely so that any condensation that might occur inside the bag can escape down the side of the stem. This is best accomplished if the 'flower' is kept in a fairly vertical attitude.

The polythene bag should be kept in place for the next week or two, until the time when the flower itself would have died and the sepals would have fallen. At that point all chance of stray pollination from another source is over and the bag can be removed. The resulting seed head will develop in the sun over the following weeks, but it could well be three to four months before it is properly mature when the seed can be collected. Do not be anxious to do this too quickly; when it is ready, the seeds will be brown, and they will fall away from each other within the cluster quite easily when ripe. It is possible to cross two varieties which do not normally flower at the same time. To do this you have to collect the pollen, on a dry, warm day, from the first variety to flower, and store it in an airtight container in a cool cupboard for use later in the year.

CUTTINGS

If you take a length of clematis vine in early summer, about 20in (50cm) long, place the bottom end in very damp peat and leave it in an unheated greenhouse, and then return a few hours later, all the leaves will have wilted and died. Shade the greenhouse and repeat the experiment. The clematis vine will again die but this time it will last much longer. Using the same shaded greenhouse, plant a shorter length of vine, about 10in (25cm). This will probably also die, but it will last much longer before doing so. Reduce the length to a single pair of leaves and it may well last over a week, or even root and grow. The larger pieces of vine die because the amount of water they lose through transpira-

tion is greater then the amount the vine can take up through its cut stem. Reducing the temperature by shading reduces the rate of transpiration, while using shorter vines reduces the leaf area to a point where the loss of moisture is virtually compensated by the intake. By reducing the moisture loss to nil, by covering with polythene or spraying with mist, a small piece of vine could be kept alive for weeks.

This very simple experiment – a good way of demonstrating to young children a plant's need for water – is useful, as it highlights an essential consideration in the management of cuttings – the need to balance the water the cuttings lose through transpiration with the amount they are able to take up through their stems, so that they can survive, develop roots, and eventually become viable. Given the right conditions, roots will grow, allowing the cutting to take up more water; this, in turn, enables it to grow, increase its total leaf area and sustain the consequent greater water loss. These are factors that the propagator must consider as he goes about his work. He will find that not all varieties will respond to the same treatment – some will need more water than others, some will need to be kept more or less close, some warmer, some colder, some will need more light, others less, and so on – so the ability to learn by experience and close attention to detail are essential. Comprehensive notes should be taken, which can be referred to year after year, giving details of both success and failure.

Cuttings are the most widely used method of propagating clematis. They are quick to do, economic with material from the parent, and result in a good plant in one to two years, which will have all the characteristics of the original. The basic equipment needed is simple, so cuttings can be made and rooted with the minimum of expense, and the small-scale propagator has the advantage in that he can keep a close eye on each of his cuttings and should be able to spot any troubles very quickly.

Most clematis varieties produce suitable

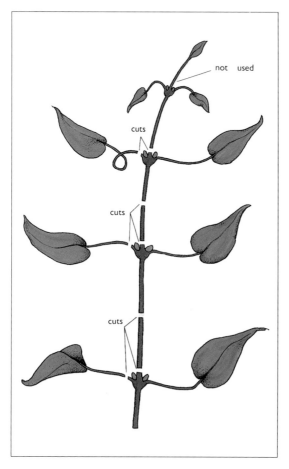

Fig 78 Length of vine from which three cuttings can be made.

material for cuttings during the spring and early summer, about mid-April to mid-July. Cuttings taken during this time make enough root and stem growth to sustain themselves during the following winter. The best cutting material will usually be the strongest growths the plant is making. These are, particularly with the summer-flowering varieties, the same growths that will produce flowers later in the season, but a proportion of such flowers must be sacrificed if cuttings are to be made. Small, weak side shoots should be ignored, as they will not root easily and are not likely to produce good plants if they do. If a length of vine is examined, it is

quite usual to find the stem is hard and woody near the base, whilst the top is green and has no real strength. It is the piece of vine between these two extremes that is of interest for cuttings, the best bits being where the stem is just starting to turn brown. This colour may vary from variety to variety but comparison between a few will identify the wood in question.

When making a cutting, the material must always be held by the stem; the leaves are easily bruised, damage which may not be apparent at the time but will show itself by the leaf starting to rot after some days in the propagator. After removing a suitable piece of vine from the parent plant, cut it into short lengths, starting each length immediately above a leaf node and finishing 1½–2in (3–4cm) below (*see* Fig 78). A very sharp knife should be used, cutting down on to a clean board, thus giving a smooth edge to the cutting and reducing the risk of introducing infection. Depending on variety, some six or seven cuttings may be possible from one vine, although some may only produce two or three. Such varieties as 'Perle d'Azur' will produce a great deal of waste wood between each cutting, others very little. You will now have a number of cuttings, together with a considerable amount of leaf.

If all the leaves are left on the cuttings they will probably fail because of transpiration. It is usual practice, therefore, to remove the leaves on one side of the cutting, and in some cases to reduce the leaf area on the other side. If the leaf is ternate (that is, made up of three parts), one or two of these parts can easily be cut off. With some varieties, and particularly when working off a mature plant, there may just be one very large leaf. This can be reduced in area simply by cutting it in half, still using the same sharp knife and board on which to cut. Only the best leaves are retained, and if all are good it might just be the position of the cutting in a tray that determines which are removed and which kept.

Close examination will show a bud in each of the leaf axils (the point where the stem joins the leaf stalk). These buds, which are always at the

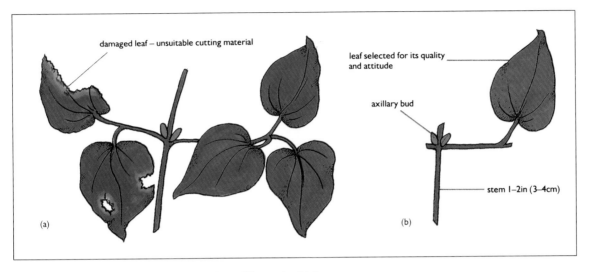

Fig 79 (a) Section of stem from which a cutting will be made. (b) An internodal cutting, from which some leaves have been removed to reduce excess leaf area.

top of the cutting – it will not grow if planted upside down – must not be damaged, as they are the only points from which a new plant can grow. Even if the cutting roots successfully, it will never grow into a plant if these buds are damaged or die. The cutting is now ready for planting.

Planting

The traditional medium into which a cutting is placed is a mixture of 50 per cent sharp sand and 50 per cent peat. The peat retains the moisture needed for growth, while the sharp sand aids drainage and helps to keep the mixture open. The peat and sand should be

Fig 80 A cutting using a simple leaf with a very large surface area.

mixed thoroughly and placed in either seed trays or small pots. The mixture needs to be quite firm in its container, otherwise the cuttings will be loose and less likely to root. The filled trays or pots should be well watered and allowed to drain before use. The cuttings are first dipped in rooting powder, in accordance with the manufacturers' instructions, and then planted. They should be pushed directly into the compost as far as the leaf stalk, the buds being just level with the surface. If the stem bends or breaks as it is inserted, throw it away – it probably wasn't mature enough. About 1 in (2·5cm) between cuttings can be used as a rough guide to spacing, although this may have to be varied if the cuttings are large or, for any reason, have an excess of leaf.

The rotting of leaves is one of the first problems to be encountered, but steps can be taken when the cuttings are first planted to reduce the chances of this. Firstly, if the cuttings are angled into the compost rather than planted with the stems vertical, it is possible to keep most of the leaf off the surface of the peat and sand – it is at this point, where leaf and compost meet, that rotting often starts. Look at the finished tray or pot of cuttings and consider how much leaf is overlapping. Some overlap cannot be avoided, but an excess may well create pockets of stagnant air between leaves, which will set off the growth of botrytis, a fluffy, grey mould which can often be found on dead, damp vegetable matter at any time of the year. A great deal of overlap suggests too much leaf is being left on the cuttings or that they are too close together. Apart from this tendency to rot from botrytis, the shaded lower leaf will not be getting light, thus reducing its effectiveness in helping the cutting to root. Similarly, if all the cuttings are angled in the same direction, there is a tendency over the following few days for the leaves, which always become slightly less turgid until roots form, to sink on to each other, again causing the same problem. A tray with the leaves all pointing in different directions is much more likely to root successfully. It will also be found from experi-

ence that rot will start on any leaves which have become damaged earlier, therefore cuttings should only be handled by their stems.

When finished, the tray of cuttings should be watered with 'Benomyl' using a watering can fitted with a fine rose. Do not allow large drops of water to drip on the tray when doing this, as the cuttings can easily be dislodged. Allow to drain and put the tray in position in your propagator. Repeat applications of 'Benomyl' are desirable, about every ten to fourteen days, if possible alternating with a different fungicide such as 'Thiram', to reduce the risk of the fungus becoming resistant to any one control.

Most varieties will root successfully without bottom heat. The Dutch have demonstrated how well this works by producing many millions of the more popular clematis each year, relying mainly on heavy shading and completing their cutting programme before midsummer – the cuttings are then left in place for about six months before they are disturbed. If bottom heat is available, the speed of rooting is increased, but this extra heat will also help to create conditions in which botrytis will flourish,

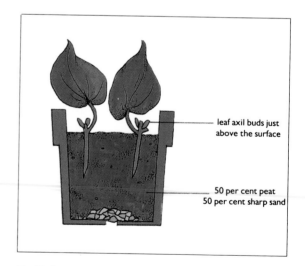

leaf axil buds just above the surface

50 per cent peat
50 per cent sharp sand

Fig 81 Internodal cuttings, which have been dipped in rooting hormone, are pushed firmly into the compost. The pot is then kept close until rooting takes place.

calling for greater vigilance in this direction. About 68°F (20°C) is the usual temperature of the propagating bed if this method is employed, although for some varieties a lower temperature may prove more suitable.

The cuttings should be kept close, either by covering with a propagator top or a sheet of polythene. One grower makes small tunnels using hoops made from 22mm plastic overflow pipe covered with polythene sheet. This works well, except that the tube expands greatly in heat, causing it to twist. Clematis cuttings also need 60 per cent shading from the sun. There are nets available of different densities which can be bought for this purpose, but usually a heavy application of greenhouse shading will suffice. Do not place your cuttings in a dark corner of a garage or garden shed and expect them to root – they do need plenty of light, but not unshaded sun.

Rooting

While they are rooting, the cuttings will have to be watched to ensure they do not dry out or become too wet. Unless mist is used, they may have to be checked three or four times a day in warm weather, and watered if they show any sign of drying out. Only practice can tell you how much water to give. If the leaves start to show signs of stress they may be too dry, and if you get much rot they could well be too wet. As they become established, you should be able to reduce the frequency of watering as the cuttings start to absorb more water from the soil through their roots. It is important to make sure that the compost does not dry out at any stage.

After Rooting

In warm weather rot may start up very quickly, so do check daily that all is well. As soon as they appear, brown patches of rot on the leaves should be cut away with a sharp pair of scissors. If this is done early, the cutting will lose only a

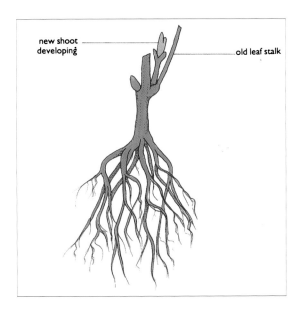

Fig 82 A well-rooted cutting.

little of its leaf and should continue to root and grow; if left, the rot will spread very quickly and many cuttings could be lost. When rooting starts, the dormant buds will break and start to grow. Do not be in too much of a hurry to pot up when you see this happening, but look down the side of the tray to see if there is a profusion of root in the compost. If not, wait a further week or two. Cuttings taken late in the season, in about July, are probably best left undisturbed until the following spring. When rooted, and this may take from as little as three weeks with some varieties to as much as three months or more with others, the cuttings can be potted into small pots using a general-purpose compost.

DIVISION

Division is the simplest method of vegetative propagation and is the easiest way of increasing stocks of herbaceous clematis varieties such as *C. integrifolia*, *C. recta* and *C. heracleifolia*. In the dormant season, ideally January or February if weather permits, the plants can be divided in

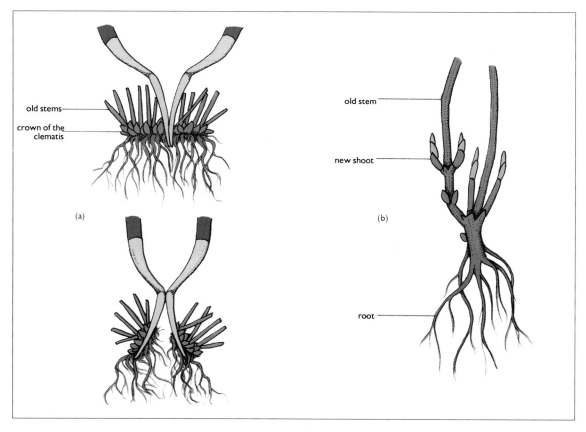

old stems

crown of the clematis

(a)

old stem

new shoot

(b)

root

Fig 83 (a) Division of herbaceous clematis in early spring, using two garden forks. (b) A section of divided plant ready for re-planting.

the same manner as any other herbaceous perennial. The clematis will have produced a clump of shoots at ground level. If the plants are very old and woody, two forks placed back to back may be used to lever the crowns apart. Smaller plants may be teased apart by hand or with a small fork or trowel. Sections of plant detached from the original should each have roots and a piece of old stem, on which there should be some visible buds. The divided clematis can then be replanted immediately in their final positions; make sure that you take exactly the same care with soil preparation as you

would with a new container-grown plant, and be certain that these young plants are on no account allowed to dry out.

If an old specimen of a non-herbaceous clematis is being moved, several stems can often be seen growing from below ground level. This is usually the result of deep planting. These individual sections, each with their own roots and shoots, may sometimes be growing in such a way that they can carefully be cut apart, and then planted out individually in the same way as you would treat new pot-grown clematis.

CHAPTER 11

Pests, Diseases and Problems

Some people who buy clematis plants do so, one suspects, on impulse, pop them into the ground with the minimum of ceremony, and then, wandering in their garden the following spring, wonder where they acquired that strange flower, before remembering their hurried purchase on a Sunday outing the year before. At the other extreme are those who suffer from what might be called 'plant hypochondria', who keep, one suspects, a 'clematis diary' rather like a hospital chart close to each plant. All leaves are inspected daily and counted, and notes are made with regard to any marks or change of colour that might occur. Leaves which show signs of anything other than radiant health are removed and sent to the path lab (the nurseryman) for clinical diagnosis. Regardless of weather conditions, water is poured on the plant daily, from a fear perhaps that, unless soaking wet, the clematis will suffer from constipation. In one case, the doctor (the nurseryman — me) was called and asked to drive fifty miles to see a plant which had been flowering happily all summer — 'I'm sure you will be as interested as we are to find out why the leaves are turning brown.' It was November at the time . . .

Fortunately, most gardeners lie somewhere between the two extremes, and can distinguish the trivia from the important, only contacting the supplier if books fail to give them the help they seek. Once established, clematis are subject to relatively few major ills. Here, we aim to distinguish between those conditions which call for action and those which do not.

LEAF DISCOLORATION

Despite the above comments, the condition of the leaves of a plant is the best indicator of its general health. Red or discoloured leaves near the bottom of a clematis are usually a sign of age in the leaf. These leaves could well be four to six months old and, often well before the plant flowers, will turn brown, die and drop off, the growing tips of the plant remaining strong and healthy. The extent to which this occurs varies from variety to variety, but 'Ville de Lyon' is particularly notorious in this respect.

Mature leaves turning yellow, with little new growth, suggest the plant is too wet. Less watering or a move to a drier site is the remedy. Pale green-yellow leaves often quickly affecting most of the plant suggest a nutrient deficiency. In the short term, feed with a liquid tomato fertiliser and then adopt the methods of feeding given on page 26.

GARDEN PESTS

Caterpillars

If your plant has leaves which are eaten round the edges, particularly from midsummer onwards, the damage is probably due to the attentions of a caterpillar of some moth or butterfly. Unless the plant is small or very badly affected, it is best to try to find the caterpillar, identify it and leave it where it is, unless it turns out to be a recognised pest. A mature clematis has more than enough leaves to sustain the odd hungry caterpillar, and leaving it to thrive on your clematis is a small price to pay for the sight of butterflies round the buddleia in August and September. It is not a good practice to get into the habit of automatically destroying all insects that cross the boundary of your property. However, if caterpillars do get out of control, a systemic insecticide containing 'Heptenophos' and 'Permethrin' will usually do the trick. Such chemicals must only be used strictly in accordance with the manufacturer's instructions.

Slugs and Snails

Huge eaten areas of leaf and stem, particularly on new shoots and early in the season, are usually due to the ravages of snails and slugs. Snails in particular can be seen high on walls from where access to a clematis is easy. Slugs will also climb, particularly up the stems, and can be found as high as 7ft (2m) or more, enjoying the new growth on the plant. The *texensis, tangutica* and *orientalis* varieties seem to be particularly prone to attack from such pests. With the *texensis* varieties, it is sometimes necessary to protect the growing tips as they come through the soil in spring with a propagator top, or something similar, for a week or two, until some height has been reached. Visual inspection and removal of such pests coupled with the use of slug bait and the encouragement of natural predators are the best controls. Keep slug bait covered, for the sake of natural predators and domestic animals.

Aphids

Curled-up leaves near the growing tips suggest some sort of aphid attack. Some varieties seem more prone to this than others, and it can be a nuisance where clematis are grown with roses or honeysuckle, both of which seem to be the first port of call for any passing greenfly. Care should be taken with insecticides, as many

customers have reported burning the tips of their clematis. Treatment is the same as that suggested for caterpillars.

Earwigs

Earwigs can be a nuisance, particularly in the autumn. They will eat round the edges of flowers, causing damage rather similar to the damage caterpillars inflict on leaves, and bore into buds before they open, thereby ruining the subsequent bloom. 'Sybol' or HCH will control this to a certain extent, but it seems impossible to eliminate it all together.

Chafer Beetle Larvae and Leather Jackets

Large established plants (and some smaller ones) can, particularly in country districts, be attacked by the larvae of the chafer beetle. This is the large beetle which, attracted by light, often flies into the house on warm nights in early summer; sometimes they are known as 'May bugs'. The larvae, which can grow to about 1½in (4cm) long, are white with a brown head. They will attack the roots of plants during the larvae stage, which, for the larger types of beetle, can last up to five years. The first the owner is likely to know about it is when his plant fails to grow in the spring or only makes very poor new growth. If dug up, the roots will be found to have been eaten back. The grubs generally inhabit old grassland and are therefore less likely to be found in urban situations. They, and leather jackets, which cause similar symptoms, can be controlled by working HCH dust into the soil round the plant, or by sprinkling some over the roots when the clematis is first planted.

Mice and Other Rodents

In our nursery greenhouses mice will eat the growing shoots off new plants, and although most survive, a percentage are lost each year due to the attentions of this pest. Mice seem to favour clematis, as it is a plant which starts into growth relatively early in the spring, when there is little other fresh vegetation about. Cats and traps are the best controls, cats usually being more effective in a garden situation, and traps being better in the greenhouse. Poison can be used but this can lead to dead and smelly mice in inaccessible places, and the risk of predators eating the poisoned animals and becoming affected.

FAILURE TO FLOWER

There are times when a clematis will make all the growth expected of it, look perfectly healthy, but not flower. Occasionally, clematis will take a year off and this, although disappointing, is nothing to worry about. If a spring or early summer variety has been pruned in the winter this will result in no early flowers, or very few (*see* Chapter 3). A very hard winter cutting back of all the previous year's growth can have the same effect. Sometimes a plant may have been labelled incorrectly by the supplier and is consequently pruned incorrectly. If this is suspected, do not prune at all and leave for one or two years to see if any flowers are produced. It should then be possible to identify the variety and adopt the correct pruning regime.

STEM PROBLEMS

The stems of clematis can easily be damaged by gales, passing animals or people. In this event, all the growth above the damage can die. When this happens, cut off all the dead growth and leave for new shoots to grow. Similarly, and particularly in new plants, very thin stems, which grow in cold spring weather, sustain huge top growths which have developed during the warmer months. If in a warm spell the plant calls for more moisture than can be sustained by the lower stem, the upper part may collapse and die, this often being mistaken for an attack

of clematis wilt. Lower shoots will develop and the plant should soon grow back to its former size. Sharply-bent stems near the base of new plants can sometimes have the same effect.

Another problem which has been seen in recent years affects montanas in particular. When the stem is damaged by, say, frost in the late spring, and the whole stem can split, there is a subsequent leakage of sap. Various bacteria and fungi will develop and grow on this, often creating some brightly coloured slimy growths. These growths will sometimes damage the structure of the stem, leading to the collapse of any of the plant beyond this point. If the main trunk is affected in a mature plant the whole clematis could be lost. Treatment consists of cutting affected growth at a point well before the point of damage and treating the wound with pruning compound.

CLEMATIS WILT

This is the most serious complaint to affect clematis. The whole of a plant, or part of it, will suddenly collapse and die, usually at a time when it is in full growth or about to flower, and particularly when humidity is high. It is now generally agreed that this is caused by a fungus, *Ascochyta*. Those parts affected should be cut off and burned. If the whole plant has been attacked to ground level, it will usually grow again, although it make take a month or two before there is any evidence of this. If planted deeply (as suggested on pages 20–24), the clematis is much more likely to survive an attack of wilt than one only planted to pot depth.

There is no sure cure or preventive measure for clematis wilt, but the incidence of it can be reduced by the use of 'Benomyl'. This should be mixed in accordance with the manufacturers' instructions for a spray, but should be watered on to the plants with a can two or three times a year. Each plant should be given about 1 gallon (5 litres) at each application, regardless of whether or not it has been attacked by wilt in the past. To reduce the risk of any infection entering the plant, it is advisable to try to keep day-to-day damage to the plant to a minimum. Keep plants well tied in to their supports, especially new growths, which are very brittle and can easily be broken in a strong wind. Ideally, broken surfaces can be treated with a good pruning compound. This regime will reduce the likelihood of your plants catching wilt and give them a much greater chance of survival. Plants that are affected will often be attacked for a number of years in succession, gradually becoming more resistant, and eventually overcoming the problem totally.

MILDEW

One of the advantages of running our clematis nursery near to the coast and about 350ft (100m) above sea level, is that there are very few still days in the course of a year, with the result that we have never seen any mildew on plants in the last ten years. Mildew is a problem that affects clematis if they are growing in sheltered positions where there is very little air movement, and seems to be more prevalent in the south of the UK. In a normal year, it is unlikely to be troublesome until after mid-summer, when it will show itself as a greyish-white powder on stems, leaves and the flowers of clematis. Apart from the colour, it will distort growth and the plant will look unhappy. Fortunately, if you are following a programme of drenching with 'Benomyl' as a precaution against wilt, you will be much less likely to come across this problem as mildew responds to the same fungicide. An alternative is 'Dinocap'.

WIND

Wind will do more damage to clematis in a short period of time than any other climatic condition. Most will survive the cold happily, unless it is coupled with a strong wind, when they can be cut down to ground level. At other times of the year, storms can shred leaves and batter flowers, break stems and generally create havoc with unprotected plants. In the wild, the clematis is usually protected by its host, the hedge. Ends of stems may be damaged and broken, but the vast majority of the plant suffers far less, as the hedge itself breaks the force of the wind. In the nursery and garden centre, this damage can be just as frustrating, with plants being broken, blown over and generally made to look unsaleable. Faced with a plant damaged in this way, the nurseryman has little choice but to cut it back and wait for it to re-grow. It is understandable, therefore, that at such points of sale a sheltered spot is usually found for clematis that are waiting to be sold. Occasionally, new plants that were in the shelter of the nursery are taken by their new owners and planted in very exposed positions without any form of shelter, twigs, and so on, to protect them while they become established. When a new plant in such a position is subjected to the full force of a gale, the leaves can be burned and the plant will look, to all intents and purposes, dead. However, if it has been planted deeply enough it will almost certainly grow again from the base, if not higher up the stem, and be none the worse for the experience. Do not be in a hurry to dig such plants out if they appear to be dead; it may well take a month or two for new growth to emerge.

DOMESTIC PETS

The attentions of domestic pets can kill your plants very easily, particularly if they return to use the same spot time and time again. One determined customer of ours is now on his fourth clematis in one spot, his dog having killed the first three!

Appendices

I LARGE-FLOWERED HYBRIDS BY COLOUR

The followings lists, which are by no means definitive, are included to facilitate the selection of clematis by colour. Full details of each variety are given in the alphabetical list in Appendix II. An asterisk after the name denotes a double or semi-double variety.

Blues, Light and Dark, Lavender and Mauve

'Alice Fisk'
'Ascotiensis'
'Beauty of Richmond'
'Beauty of Worcester'*
'Countess of Lovelace'*
'Daniel Deronda'*
'Elsa Spath'
'H. F. Young'
'General Sikorski'
'Glynderek'*
'Ken Donson'
'Lady Caroline Nevill'*
'Lady Northcliffe'
'Lasurstern'
'Lawsoniana'
'Louise Rowe'*
'Lord Nevill'
'Mrs Cholmondeley'
'Mrs Hope'
'Mrs P. B. Truax'
'Perle d'Azur'
'Prince Charles'
'Ramona'
'Violet Charm'
'Vyvyan Pennell'*

'W. E. Gladstone'
'Will Goodwin'
'William Kennett'

Violet and Purple

'Gipsy Queen'
'Haku Ookan'
'Jackmanii'
'Jackmanii Superba'
'Lady Betty Balfour'
'Mme Grange'
'Royalty'*
'The President'
'Warsaw Nike'

Mauve and Rosy-Purple

'Horn of Plenty'
'Kathleen Dunford'*
'Richard Pennell'
'Ruby Glow'
'Victoria'

Red

'Allanah'
'Cardinal Wyszynski'
'Crimson King'
'Duchess of Sutherland'
'Ernest Markham'
'Jackmanii Rubra'*
'Mme Edouard André'
'Niobe'
'Rouge Cardinal'
'Ville de Lyon'
'Voluceau'

Fig 84 A popular variety named after its hybridiser, 'Ernest Markham'. This one dates back to 1926.

Pink and Mauve-Pink

'Asao'
'Comtesse de Bouchaud'
'Dorothy Walton'
'Hagley Hybrid'
'Mme Baron Veillard'
'Margaret Hunt'
'Miss Crawshay'*
'Mrs Spencer Castle'*
'Proteus'*
'Walter Pennell'*

White and Pastel Shades

'Belle of Woking'*
'Dawn'

'Duchess of Edinburgh'*
'Henryi'
'Jackmanii Alba'*
'John Huxtable'
'Lady Londesborough'
'Marie Boisselot'
'Miss Bateman'
'Mrs George Jackman'*
'Sylvia Denny'*
'Wada's Primrose'

Striped Clematis

Predominantly Mauve/Lavender

'Barbara Jackman'
'Bracebridge Star'
'Joan Picton'
'Saturn'
'Sealand Gem'

Predominantly Pink

'Bee's Jubilee'
'Capitaine Thuilleaux'
'Carnaby'
'Charissima'
'Dr Ruppel'
'John Warren'
'King George V'
'Lincoln Star'
'Marcel Moser'
'Nelly Moser'
'Pink Fantasy'
'Scartho Gem'

Predominantly Violet-Purple

'Mrs N. Thompson'
'Serenata'
'Sir Garnet Wolseley'
'Star of India'
'Wilhemina Tull'

Predominantly Purplish-Red

'Barbara Dibley'
'Corona'
'Myojo'

Predominantly White

'Fairy Queen'
'Fair Rosamund'
'John Paul II'

11 CLEMATIS VARIETIES

To assist readers when choosing clematis we have listed most of the better-known clematis

Fig 85 'Mrs N. Thompson', a richly-coloured variety which can take some time to become established.

Fig 86 'Fairy Queen', an old variety which can, in a sheltered spot, go on flowering until Christmas.

that are available from one or other of the specialist nurseries in Great Britian. Throughout the world there are many hundreds of different hybrids and species, to which more are being added each year by both hybridisation and new discoveries in the field. A great many of the unlisted species varieties are either unsuited to garden cultivation or have insignificant flowers and are usually only sought by collectors. With many of the large-flowered varieties the differences between one variety and another can be very slight, and so nurseries may not stock both. With these similarities it is always worth asking a supplier if he can suggest an alternative if the variety which you are seeking is out of stock.

113

Large-Flowered Varieties

VARIETY	DESCRIPTION	FLOWERING MONTHS	PRUNING CODE	HEIGHT	PLANTING ASPECT
Allanah	Bright red, dark brown stamens 6–8in (15–20cm) dia.	6 to 9	3	7–8¾ft (2–2·5m)	E, S, W
Alice Fisk	Wisteria-blue flower, 6–8in (15–20cm) dia. Edges crenulated, brown stamens.	5, 6, 9	2	7–8¾ft (2–2·5m)	Any
Asao	Deep pink, slightly darker around edges of sepals. 6in (15cm) dia.	5, 6, 9	2	8¾–10½ft (2·5–3m)	Any
Barbara Dibley	Petunia red, carmine bars and dark centre. 6–8in (15–20cm) dia.	5, 6, 9	2	8¾–14ft (2·5–4m)	E, S, W
Barbara Jackman	Mauve with crimson bar, stamens cream, 5–7in (12–18cm) dia.	5, 6, 9	2	8¾–14ft (2·5–4m)	Any
Bee's Jubilee	Mauve-pink with carmine bar, 6–8in (15–20cm) dia. Very like Nelly Moser.	5, 6, 9	2	8¾–14ft (2·5–4m)	Any
Beauty of Richmond	Large pale lavender-blue flower, up to 10in (25cm) dia. Stamens brown.	5, 6, 9	2	12¼–14ft (3·5–4m)	Any
Beauty of Worcester	Deep blue double flower, single flowers in autumn. 6–8in (15–20cm) dia.	5, 6, 9	2	8¾–14ft (2·5–4m)	E, S, W
Belle of Woking	Silver-grey double, rosette-shaped 4–6in (10–15cm) dia.	5, 6, 9	2	8¾–14ft (2·5–4m)	E, S, W
Bracebridge Star	Lavender-blue with carmine bars and pointed sepals 6–8in (15–20cm) dia.	5, 6, 9	2	8¾–14ft (2·5–4m)	E, N, W
Capitaine Thuilleaux	Deep pink bars on a cream background 6–8in (15–20cm) dia.	5, 6, 9	2	8¾–14ft (2·5–4m)	E, N, W
Cardinal Wyszynski	Crimson with gold stamens 6–8in (15–20cm) dia.	6 to 9	3	8¾–14ft (2·5–4m)	E, S, W
Carnaby	Deep pink with darker bar, 6in (15cm) dia. A compact plant.	5 and 6	2	8¾–14ft (2–2·5m)	E, N, W
Charissima	Cerise-pink with deeper bar, 8–10in (20–25cm) dia.	6 to 9	2	8¾–10½ft (2·5–3m)	Any
Comtesse de Bouchaud	Mauve-pink flowers, 4–6in (10–15cm) dia. with cream stamens. Very vigorous.	6 to 9	3	8¾–14ft (2·5–4m)	Any
Corona	Bright purplish-pink sepals and dark red anthers. 6–8in (15–20cm)	5, 6, 9	2	8¾–10½ft (2·5–3m)	Any
Countess of Lovelace	Lavender blue, double and single flowers 6–8in (15–20cm) dia., white stamens.	6 to 9	2	8¾–14ft (2·5–4m)	Any
Crimson King	Rich wine-red sepals, brown stamens, 6–8in (15–20cm) dia.	6 to 9	2	8¾–14ft (2·5–4m)	E, S, W

VARIETY	DESCRIPTION	FLOWERING MONTHS	PRUNING CODE	HEIGHT	PLANTING ASPECT
Daniel Deronda	Deep violet-blue with yellow stamens, 6–8in (15–20cm) dia. Spring flowers semi-double, single later. Avoid a windy site.	6 to 10	2	8¾–14ft (2·5–4m)	Any
Dawn	Pearly-pink. 6–8in (15–20cm) dia. Compact, similar to Miss Bateman but more frost hardy.	5, 6, 9	2	8¾–14ft (2·5–4m)	E, N, W
Dorothy Walton	Long pointed mauve-pink sepals, brown stamens, 4–6in (10–15cm) dia. Flowers freely.	6 to 9	3	14–17½ft (4–5m)	E, S, W
Dr Ruppel	Rose-pink with carmine bar, 6–8in (15–20cm) dia.	5, 6, 9	2	8¾–14ft (2·5–4m)	Any
Duchess of Edinburgh	White rosette-shaped double flowers, stamens yellow, 4–6in (10–15cm) dia.	5, 6, 9	2	8¾–14ft (2·5–4m)	Any
Duchess of Sutherland	Mid-red with lighter bar and golden stamens. Flower dia. 5–7in (12–18cm)	6 to 9	2	8¾–14ft (2·5–4m)	E, S, W
Elsa Spath (Syn. Xerxes)	Deep violet-blue overlapping sepals, red stamens, 6–8in (15–20cm) dia.	6 to 9	2	7–8¾ft (2–2·5m)	E, S, W
Ernest Markham	Glowing petunia-red sepals, gold stamens 6–8in (15–20cm) dia. Will flower on old wood.	7 to 10	3	8¾–17½ft (4–5m)	E, S, W
Fairy Queen	Flesh-coloured, almost white sepals with light rose bar, 6–8in (15–20cm) dia.	6, 7, 8	2	8¾–14ft (3·5–4m)	E or W
Fair Rosamond	Red bar on white background, slightly scented. Purple stamens. 4–6in (10–15cm)	6 to 9	2	8¾–14ft (2·5–4m)	E, S, W
General Sikorski	Mid-blue with reddish tinge, edges of sepals crenulated. Stamens golden, 6–8in (15–20cm) dia.	6, 7, 8	2	8¾–14ft (2·5–4m)	E, S, W
Gipsy Queen	Deep violet purple flowers, velvety surface. Stamens red, 4–6in (10–15cm) dia.	8, 9, 10	3	14–22¾ft (4–6·5m)	E, S, W
Glynderek	Deep double blue early, single later. Dark stamens. 6–8in (15–20cm) dia.	5, 6, 9	2	8¾–14ft (2·5–4m)	E, S, W
Hagley Hybrid	Shell-pink sepals contrast with dark stamens, 4–6in (10–15cm) dia. Vigorous, best out of sun.	6 to 9	3	7–8¾ft (2–2·5m)	Any
Haku Ookan	An unusual striking variety from Japan. Violet sepals with contrasting white stamens. 6–8in (15–20cm) dia.	5, 6, 9	2	8¾–14ft (2·5–4m)	E, S, W
Henryi	A creamy-white flower, pointed sepals and dark stamens. Flowers 6–8in (15–20cm) dia.	6 to 9	2	14–22¾ft (4–6·5m)	Any
H. F. Young	Wedgwood blue flower, stamens cream, a compact variety with a great deal of flower, 6–8in (15–20cm) dia.	5, 6, 9	2	8¾–14ft (2·5–4m)	E, S, W

VARIETY	DESCRIPTION	FLOWERING MONTHS	PRUNING CODE	HEIGHT	PLANTING ASPECT
Horn of Plenty	Rosy-mauve, deep-coloured, red centre. Large attractive flower 8–10in (20–25cm) dia.	5, 6, 9	2	8¾–14ft (2·5–4m)	Any
Jackmanii	Purple sepals, greenish stamens, masses of flowers. 4–6in (10–15cm) dia.	6 to 9	3	14–22¾ft (4–6·5m)	Any
Jackmanii Alba	Bluish-white, semi-double on old wood. 4–6in (10–15cm) dia.	6 to 9	2 or 3	14–22¾ft (4–6·5m)	Any
Jackmanii Rubra	Petunia-red with cream stamens. Can be double if left unpruned. 4–6in (10–15cm) dia.	6 to 9	2	14–22¾ft (4–6·5m)	E, S, W
Jackmanii Superba	Perhaps the most popular. Deep violet-blue flowers slightly wider sepals than Jackmanii.	6 to 9	3	14–22¾ft (4–6·5m)	Any
Joan Picton	Lilac with light bar. Brown stamens. 6–8in (15–20cm) dia. A compact, free-flowering variety.	5, 6, 9	2	8¾–14ft (2·5–4m)	Any
John Huxtable	White with cream stamens. 4–6in (10–15cm) dia. Similar to Comtesse de Bouchaud in habit.	6 to 9	3	8¾–14ft (2·5–4m)	Any
John Paul II	Off-white with pink tinge which sometimes develops into a bar later in the season. Vigorous. 4–6in (10–15cm) dia.	6 to 9	2	14–17½ft (4–5m)	Any
John Warren	Pointed overlapping French-grey sepals with deep carmine edges. Brown stamens. 6–8in (15–20cm) dia. A compact variety.	6 to 9	2	7–10½ft (2–3m)	E, S, W
Kathleen Dunford	Semi-double. Rosy-purple and golden stamens. Single in autumn. 6–8in (15–20cm) dia.	5, 6, 9	2	8¾–14ft (2·5–4m)	E, S, W
Kathleen Wheeler	Large plummy-mauve flowers with golden stamens. 8–10in (20–25cm) dia.	6 to 9	2	8¾–14ft (2·5–4m)	Any
Ken Donson	Deep blue with golden stamens. 6–8in (15–20cm) dia.	6 to 9	2	8¾–14ft (2·5–4m)	Any
King George V	Pink with dark bar. 6–8in (15–20cm) dia.	7 and 8	2	8¾–14ft (2·5–4m)	E or W
Lady Betty Balfour	Violet-blue with yellow stamens. A very late variety which needs full sun. 6–8in (15–20cm) dia.	9 and 10	3	14–22¾ft (4–6·5m)	S
Lady Caroline Nevill	Semi-double in spring. Lavender-blue flowers, beige stamens, 6–8in (15–20cm) dia.	6 to 10	2	14–22¾ft (4–6·5m)	E, S, W
Lady Londesborough	Pale mauve-blue turning to silver-grey. Dark stamens. One of the earliest of the large-flowered varieties. 6–8in (15–20cm) dia.	5, 6, 9	2	8¾–14ft (2·5–4m)	E, S, W
Lady Northcliffe	Lavender-blue flowers, compact grower. 4–6in (10–15cm) dia.	6 to 9	2	7–8¾ft (2–2·5m)	E, S, W

VARIETY	DESCRIPTION	FLOWERING MONTHS	PRUNING CODE	HEIGHT	PLANTING ASPECT
Lasurstern	Pointed lavender-blue sepals, wavy edges; cream stamens. 6½–9in (16–22cm) dia.	5, 6, 9	2	8¾–14ft (2·5–4m)	E, S, W
Lawsoniana	Long lavender-blue sepals with a red tint. Stamens brown. 8–10in (20–25cm) dia.	6 to 9	2	14–17½ft (4–5m)	E, S, W
Lilacina Floribunda	Rich purple. Floriferous. Flower diameter 6–8in (15–20cm).	7, 8, 9	3	14–17½ft (4–5m)	Any
Lincoln Star	Long pointed raspberry-pink sepals. Late flowers paler but with a darker bar, 6–8in (15–20cm) dia.	5, 6, 9	2	8¾–14ft (2·5–4m)	E, N, W
Lord Nevill	Deep blue sepals with crenulated edges. Bluish-purple stamens. 6–8in (15–20cm) dia.	5 to 9	2	8¾–14ft (2·5–4m)	S or W
Louise Rowe	Pale-mauve with golden stamens. Flowers double, semi-double and single all at same time. 6–8in (15–20cm) dia.	6, 7, 9	2	7–8¾ft (2–2·5m)	E, S, W
Madame Baron Veillard	Pointed lilac-rose sepals. 4–6in (10–15cm) dia.	9 and 10	3	14–17½ft (4–5m)	S or W
Madame Edouard André	Deep red pointed sepals, cream stamens. Flowers 4–6in (10–15cm) dia.	6 to 9	3	7–8¾ft (2–2·5m)	E, S, W
Madame Grange	Dusky purple with silver reverse. Dark red-brown stamens. 4–6in (10–15cm) dia.	8, 9, 10	3	8¾–14ft (2·4–4m)	E, S, W
Marcel Moser	Light mauve-pink sepals with deeper bar. 7–8in (18–20cm) dia.	5, 6, 9	2	8¾–14ft (2·5–4m)	Any
Margaret Hunt	Dusky pink-mauve flowers, 4–6in (10–15cm) dia. A vigorous and free-flowering variety.	6 to 9	3	8¾–22¾ft (4–6·5m)	Any
Marie Boisselot (Syn. Mme le Coultre)	Pure white with yellow stamens. Beautiful and free-flowering; blooms held horizontally. 6–8in (15–20cm) dia.	6 to 9	2	8¾–22¾ft (4–6·5m)	Any
Maureen	Rich purple, 6–8in (15–20cm) dia.	6 to 9	2	7–8¾ft (2–2·5m)	E, S, W
Miss Bateman	Creamy-white with chocolate-red stamens. Free-flowering. 4–6in (10–15cm) dia.	5, 6, 9	2	7–8¾ft (2–2·5m)	Any
Miss Crawshay	Rosy-mauve, fawn stamens. Semi-double in Spring. 4–6in (10–15cm) dia.	6 to 9	2	8¾–14ft (2·5–4m)	E, S, W
Mrs Cholmondeley	Large lavender-blue flowers with chocolate stamens. A long flowering season. 6½–9in (16–22cm) dia.	5 to 9	2	14–17½ft (4–5m)	Any
Mrs George Jackman	Double. Creamy-white flowers 6–18in (15–20cm) dia.	6 to 9	2	7–8¾ft (2–2·5m)	E, S, W
Mrs Hope	Well-shaped light blue flower with red stamens. Vigorous grower. 6–8in (15–20cm) dia.	7 to 9	2	14–17½ft (4–5m)	S or W

VARIETY	DESCRIPTION	FLOWERING MONTHS	PRUNING CODE	HEIGHT	PLANTING ASPECT
Mrs N. Thompson	Deep violet with vivid scarlet bar and purple-red stamens. Very striking. 4–6in (10–15cm) dia.	5, 6, 9	2	8¾–14ft (2·5–4m)	E, S, W
Mrs P. B. Truax	Light blue, cream stamens. A compact grower. 4–6in (10–15cm) dia.	5 and 6	2	7–10½ft (2–3m)	E, S, W
Mrs Spencer Castle	Pale mauve-pink double flowers in early summer, single in late summer. 4–6in (10–15cm) dia.	5, 6, 9	2	14–17½ft (4–5m)	Any
Myojo	Velvety-red with deeper bar. Predominant cream stamens. 6–8in (15–20cm) dia.	5, 6, 9	2	8¾–10½ft (2·5–3m)	Any
Nelly Moser	Pale mauve-pink with deep carmine bar. Hardy and vigorous. Fades badly in full sun but fine in shade. 7–9in (18–22cm) dia.	5, 6, 9	2	8¾–14ft (2·5–4m)	E, N, W
Niobe	Deep ruby-red, almost black on first opening. Pointed sepals and yellow stamens. 6–8in (15–20cm) dia.	6 to 9	2 or 3	8¾–14ft (2·5–4m)	E, S, W
Perle d'Azur	Sky-blue, semi-nodding flowers with six broad, blunt-tipped, corrugated sepals. Flowers freely. 4–6in (10–15cm) dia.	7 to 10	3	12¼–17½ft (2·5–5m)	Any
Pink Fantasy	Pale pink with darker bar. Brown stamens. 4–6in (10–15cm) dia.	6 to 9	3	7–8¾ft (2–2·5m)	E, S, W
Proteus	Mauve-pink double, 6–8in (15–20cm) dia. Single in autumn.	5, 6, 9	2	12¼–14ft (3·5–4m)	E or W
Prince Charles	Masses of mauve-blue medium-sized flowers, 4–6in (10–15cm) dia.	6 to 9	3	5¼–7ft (1·5–2m)	E, S, W
Ramona (Syn. Hybrida Seiboldii)	Large lavender-blue flowers with slightly reflexed sepals and dark stamens. 6–8in (15–20cm) dia.	6 to 9	2	12¼–17½ft (3·5–5m)	Any
Richard Pennell	Purple-blue with gold and red stamens. 6–8in (15–20cm) dia.	6 to 8	2	8¾–14ft (2·5–4m)	Any
Rouge Cardinal	Velvety, crimson flowers with rounded sepals and brown stamens. 4–6in (10–15cm) dia. Needs a sunny site.	6 to 9	3	7–8¾ ft (2–2·5m)	E, S, W
Royalty	Free-flowering, semi-double with purple-mauve sepals and yellow anthers. 6–8in (15–20cm) dia.	5, 6, 9	2	8¾–10½ft (2·5–3m)	E, S, W
Ruby Glow	Glowing rosy-purple flowers, 6–8in (15–20cm) dia.	6 to 9	2	8¾–14ft (2·5–4m)	E, S, W
Saturn	Lavender-blue with maroon bar and white stamens with dark tips. Vigorous. 6–8in (15–20cm) dia.	5, 6, 9	2	8¾–14ft (2·5–4m)	E, S, W

VARIETY	DESCRIPTION	FLOWERING MONTHS	PRUNING CODE	HEIGHT	PLANTING ASPECT
Scartho Gem	Bright pink with deeper bar. Flowers in great profusion. 6–8in (15–20cm) dia.	6 to 9	2	8¾–14ft (2·5–4m)	Any
Sealand Gem	Rosy-mauve with darker pink bar and brown stamens. Very free-flowering. 4–6in (10–15cm) dia.	6 to 9	2	8¾·14ft (2·5–4m)	Any
Serenata	Dusky purple, yellow stamens. 4–6in (10–15cm) dia.	6 to 9	2	8¾–14ft (2·5–4m)	Any
Sir Garnet Wolseley	Mauve-blue sepals with darker bar. 6–8in (15–20cm) dia.	5, 6, 8	2	8¾–12½ft (2·5–3·5m)	E, S, W
Snow Queen	White with blue tint and brown stamens. Sometimes pink bars in autumn. 6–8in (15–20cm) dia.	5, 6, 9	2	7–8¾ft (2–2·5m)	E, S, W
Star of India	Free-flowering, deep purple with carmine bar. 3–5in (8–12cm) dia.	6 to 9	3	14–17½ft (4–5m)	Any
Sylvia Denny	Medium-sized double white flower with pale yellow anthers. 4–6in (10–15cm) dia.	5, 6, 9	2	8¾–14ft (2·5–4m)	E, S, W
The President	Rich purple-blue sepals with reddish-brown stamens. Very long flowering period. 6–8in (15–20cm) dia.	6 to 9	2	8¾–14ft (2·5–4m)	Any
Twilight	Petunia-mauve sepals with yellow stamens. Very free-flowering. 6–8in (15–20cm) dia.	6 to 9	2	8¾–14ft (2·5–4m)	E, S, W
Victoria	Rosy-purple fading to mauve. Brown stamens. 4–6in (10–15cm) dia.	6 to 9	3	12½–17½ft (3·5–5m)	Any
Ville de Lyon	Rounded flowers, carmine-red shading to deep crimson round the edges of the sepals. Golden stamens. Needs a sunny position. 4–6in (10–15cm) dia.	7 to 10	3	8¾–14ft (2·5–4m)	E, S, W
Violet Charm	Pointed violet sepals, crimped edges, brown stamens. 6–8in (15–20cm) dia.	6 to 9	2	7–8¾ft (2–2·5m)	E, S, W
Voluceau	Petunia-red, rather twisted sepals with contrasting yellow stamens. Very free-flowering. 4–6in (10–15cm) dia.	6 to 9	3	8¾–14ft (2·5–4m)	E, S, W
Vyvyan Pennell	Violet-blue shaded with crimson, rosette-shaped double flowers in spring. Deep lavender-blue single flowers in autumn. 6–8in (15–20cm) dia.	5, 6, 9	2	8¾–14ft (2·5–4m)	E, S, W
Wada's Primrose	Creamy-white with deeper bar and yellow stamens. 6–8in (15–20cm) dia.	5 and 6	2	8¾–22½ft (2·5–6·5m)	E or W
Warsaw Nike	Rich royal purple with golden anthers. Free-flowering. 6–8in (15–20cm) dia.	6 to 9	2	8¾–10½ft (2·5–3m)	E, S, W

Fig 87 'Vyvyan Pennell', one of the most popular double varieties.

Fig 88 This native of China, the evergreen Clematis paniculata, must be kept frost free and is best suited to a conservatory or glasshouse.

VARIETY	DESCRIPTION	FLOWERING MONTHS	PRUNING CODE	HEIGHT	PLANTING ASPECT
W. E. Gladstone	Pointed lavender sepals and red stamens. One of the largest flowers. 8–10in (20–25cm) dia.	6 to 9	2	12½–17½ft (3·5–5m)	E, S, W
Will Goodwin	Lavender-blue with crenulated edges, golden stamens. 6–8in (15–20cm) dia.	6 to 9	2	8¾–14ft (2·5–4m)	E, S, W
William Kennett	Deep lavender-blue flowers and dark red stamens. The overlapping sepals have crimped edges. 6–8in (15–20cm) dia.	6 to 9	2	35–70ft (10–20m)	Any

Small-Flowered Varieties and Species

VARIETY	DESCRIPTION	FLOWERING MONTHS	PRUNING CODE	HEIGHT	PLANTING ASPECT
C. alpina 'Burford White'	Very free-flowering, pure white lantern-shaped flowers. 1–2in (2–5cm) dia.	4 and 5	1	7–8¾ft (2–2.5m)	Any
C. alpina 'Frances Rivis'	The largest *alpina*. Mid-blue lantern flowers, white stamens. 1–2½in (2–6cm) dia.	4 and 5	1	7–8¾ft (2–2.5m)	Any
C. alpina 'Pamela Jackman'	A rich mid-blue variety with broad tapering sepals. Hardy. 1–2in (2–5cm) dia.	4 and 5	1	7–8¾ft (2–2.5m)	Any
C. alpina 'Ruby'	Red nodding flowers with white stamens. 1–2in (2–5cm) dia.	4 and 5	1	7–8¾ft (2–2.5m)	Any
C. alpina 'Willy'	Pale pink variety with reddish base to sepals and white petaloid stamens. 1–2in (2–5cm) dia.	4 and 5	1	7–8¾ft (2–2.5m)	Any
C. apiifolia	A deciduous variety from Japan. Tiny white four-sepalled flowers.	8	3	12¼–14ft (3.5–4m)	Any
C. armandii	Large, glossy evergreen leaves and white scented flowers. A Chinese variety needing the protection of a sheltered wall or cold greenhouse. Flowers 1–2in (2–5cm) in clusters.	3 and 4	1	24½–35ft (7–10m)	S or W
C. calycina	*See C. cirrhosa.*				
C. chrysocoma sericea (syn. spooneri)	Pure white flowers with yellow stamens. A strong grower of the *montana* type. Flowers 2–3in (5–8cm) dia.	5 and 6	1	24½–35ft (7–10m)	Any
C. cirrhosa var. Balearica (syn. C. balearica, c. calycina)	Finely cut evergreen leaves that turn bronze in winter. Small, bell-shaped yellow flowers, spotted reddish-purple within. Needs a sheltered sunny position.	1 to 3	1	24½–35ft (7–10m)	S or W
C. cirrhosa 'Wisley Cream'	Leaves paler than *cirrhosa*. Cream flowers, no freckles.				
C. connata	A Himalayan variety. Small bell-shaped scented yellow flowers. Somewhat similar to *rehderiana*.	9 and 10	3	24½–28ft (7–8m)	Any
C. eriostemon	Nodding purple flowers similar to *viticella* but larger. Non-clinging habit. Flowers 1–2in (2–5cm) dia.	7 to 10	3	12¼–17½ft (3.5–5m)	E, S, W
C. fargesii var. 'Soulei'	A vigorous species. White flowers in clusters. 1½in (4cm) dia.	7 to 9	3	14–17½ft (4–5m)	Any

VARIETY	DESCRIPTION	FLOWERING MONTHS	PRUNING CODE	HEIGHT	PLANTING ASPECT
C. flammula	Masses of highly-scented, white star-like flowers followed by silver-grey seed heads. Flowers ½–1in (1–2cm) dia.	8 to 10	3	24½–35ft (7–10m)	E, S, W
C. florida 'Sieboldii' (syn. 'Bicolor')	A delicate variety often mistaken for a passion flower. White outer sepals, purple centre. 3–4in (8–10cm) dia.	6 to 9	3	7–10½ft (2–3m	S or protect
C. florida 'Alba Plena'	All-white form of *florida* 'Sieboldii'.	6 to 9	3	7–10½ft (2–3m)	S or protect
C. forsteri	Evergreen from New Zealand. Flowers creamy-yellow star-shaped, ½–1in (1–2cm) dia. scented.	4 and 5	1	10½–14ft (3–4m)	Frost free
C. fusca	Vigorous herbaceous species. Pitcher-shaped red-brown flowers, ½–1in (1–2cm) dia.	6	3	7–8¾ft (2–2.5m)	E, S, W
C. glauca	Orange-yellow, similar to *orientalis* but with glaucous, thinly-cut leaves.	7 and 8	2 or 3	17½–24½ft (5–7m)	E, S, W
C. glauca var. 'Akebioides'	Silvery leaves, small yellow flowers with dark centres.	7 and 8	2 or 3	17½–21ft (5–6m)	E, S, W
C. heracleifolia 'Campanile'	Herbaceous variety, coarse leaves, clusters of small, pale blue flowers each about ½–¾in (1–1.5cm) dia.	8 to 9	3	2½–3½ft (75–100cm)	Herbaceous border
C. heracleifolia 'Davidiana'	Similar to 'Campanile' but scented.	8 to 9	3	2½–3½ft (75–100cm)	Herbaceous border
C. heracleifolia 'Mrs Robert Brydon'	Off-white scented version of the type.	8 to 9	3	2½–3½ft (75–100cm)	Herbaceous border
C. heracleifolia 'Wyevale'	A blue version of the type, scented.	8 to 9	3	2½–3½ft (75–100cm)	Herbaceous border
C. huldine	Pearly-white flower with mauve bars on reverse of sepals. A vigorous variety, free-flowering. 3–4in (8–10cm) dia.	7 to 10	3	14–22¾ft (4–6.5m)	E, S, W
C. integrifolia	Small, nodding, indigo-blue flowers. Herbaceous.	7	3	2½–3½ft (75–100cm)	Any
C. integrifolia 'Durandii'	A semi-herbaceous variety to grow through a small shrub. Rich indigo-blue deeply-ribbed sepals with off-white stamens. 3–4in (8–10cm) dia.	6 to 9	3	7–8¾ft (2–2.5m)	E, S, W
C. integrifolia 'Hendersonii'	Larger-flowered version of the type. Flowers up to 2in (5cm) dia. bell-shaped, blue with long stems.	6 to 9	3	2½–3½ft (75–100cm)	Herbaceous border
C. integrifolia 'Olgae'	Pale blue version with twisted sepals and sweet scent.	6 to 9	3	2½–3½ft (75–100cm)	Herbaceous border

VARIETY	DESCRIPTION	FLOWERING MONTHS	PRUNING CODE	HEIGHT	PLANTING ASPECT
C. integrifolia 'Rosea'	Pink flowers, darker on reverse, similar shape to 'Olgae'. Scented.	6 to 9	3	2½–3½ft (75–100cm)	Herb-aceous border
C. jouiniana	Masses of small, soft blue hyacinth-like flowers, ½–1in (1–2cm) dia. Semi-herbaceous, useful as ground cover or to grow over a tree stump.	9 and 10	2 or 3	12¼–22¾ft (2·5–6·5m)	E, S, W
C. jouiniana 'Praecox'	Pale purple-pink variety with an earlier flowering period.	8 to 10	2 or 3	12¼–22¾ft (3·5–6·5m)	E, S, W
C. macropetala	Lavender-blue nodding flowers, semi-double with white stamens. 1½–2in (4–5cm) dia.	4 and 5	1	8¾–12¼ft (2·5–3·5m)	Any
C. macropetala 'Blue Bird'	Larger version of *macropetala*.	4 and 5	1	8¾–12¼ft (2·5–3·5m)	Any
C. macropetala 'Jan Lindmark'	Excellent mauve variety from Sweden.	4 and 5	1	8¾–12¼ft (2·5–3·5m)	Any
C. macropetala 'Maidwell Hall'	Deeper blue version of *macropetala*.	4 and 5	1	8¾–12¼ft (2·5–3·5m)	Any
C. macropetala 'Markham's Pink'	Pink form of *macropetala*.	4 and 5	1	8¾–12¼ft (2·5–3·5m)	Any
C. macropetala 'Rosy O'Grady'	A deep pink form of *macropetala*.	4 and 5	1	8¾–12¼ft (2·5–3·5m)	Any
C. macropetala 'Snow Bird'	White form, slightly later flowering.	5	1	8¾–12¼ft (2·5–3·5m)	Any
C. macropetala 'White Moth'	Small nodding double white flowers with tapering sepals. 1–2in (2–5cm) dia.	4 and 5	1	7–8¾ft (2–2·5m)	Any
C. macropetala 'White Swan'	White form of *macropetala*.	4 and 5	1	8¾–12¼ft (2·5–3·5m)	Any
C. maximowicziana	Small, white, scented flowers. Needs good summer in UK.	9 and 10	3	17½–21ft (5–6m)	S
C. montana	A multitude of pure white blooms 2in (5cm) dia.	5 and 6	1	24½–35ft (7–10m)	Any
C. montana 'Alexander'	Creamy-white scented flowers, 2–2½in (5–6cm) dia.	5 and 6	1	24½–35ft (7–10m)	Any
C. montana 'Elizabeth'	Soft pink flowers, 2–2½in (5–6cm) dia. Sweetly scented.	5 and 6	1	24½–35ft (7–10m)	Any
C. montana 'Freda'	Deep pink with darker edges to sepals. 2–2½in (5–6cm) dia. Bronzy foliage.	5 and 6	1	24½–35ft (7–10m)	Any
C. montana 'Marjorie'	Double. Coppery-pink with darker pink stamens. 2in (5cm) dia.	5 and 6	1	24½–35ft (7–10m)	Any
C. montana 'Mayleen'	Deep pink with golden stamens, 2–3in (5–8cm) dia. Bronzy foliage.	5 and 6	1	24½–35ft (7–10m)	Any
C. montana 'Picton's Variety'	Deep pink flowers, more compact than other montanas. 2–2½in (5–6cm) dia.	5 and 6	1	14–17½ft (4–5m)	Any
C. montana 'Pink Perfection'	Similar to 'Elizabeth' but a deeper pink. 2–2½in (5–6cm) dia.	5 and 6	1	24½–35ft (7–10m)	Any

Fig 89 The largest of the montana *varieties,* C. montana *'Tetrarose'.*

VARIETY	DESCRIPTION	FLOWERING MONTHS	PRUNING CODE	HEIGHT	PLANTING ASPECT
C. montana rubens	Deep pink with golden stamens and dark foliage. Very popular. Flowers 2–2½in (5–6cm) dia.	5 and 6	1	24½–35ft (7–10m)	Any
C. montana 'Tetrarose'	Large lilac-rose flowers with rich bronzy-green foliage. 2–3in (5–8cm) dia.	5 and 6	1	24½–35ft (7–10m)	Any
C. orientalis	Orange-yellow nodding flowers 1–3in (2–4cm) dia. Finely-cut foliage. Attractive seed heads.	7 to 10	2 or 3	12¼–22¾ft (3·5–6·5m)	E, S, W
C. orientalis 'Bill MacKenzie'	The largest of the *orientalis* varieties. Deep yellow flowers about 2–2½in (5–6cm) dia.	7 to 10	2 or 3	12¼–22¾ft (3·5–6·5m)	E, S, W
C. orientalis 'Burford Variety'	An *orientalis/tangutica* cross. Deep yellow flowers with thick sepals.	7 to 10	2 or 3	17½–24½ft (5–7m)	E, S, W
C. orientalis 'Corry'	A Dutch hybrid with pale yellow flowers.	7 to 10	2 or 3	17½–24½ft (5–7m)	E, S, W

VARIETY	DESCRIPTION	FLOWERING MONTHS	PRUNING CODE	HEIGHT	PLANTING ASPECT
C. paniculata	Evergreen from New Zealand with white sepals and pink anthers. 1–1½in (2–3cm) dia. Dioecious. Male plant more spectacular. Brown spots on leaves of female.	5	1	14–17½ft (4–5m)	Frost free
C. recta	Herbaceous. Masses of small creamy-white flowers. Scented. ¼–½in (0·5–1cm) dia.	6, 7, 8	3	2½–3½ft (75–100cm)	Any
C. recta '**Purpurea**'	Purple-leaved form of *C. recta*.	6, 7, 8	3	2½–3½ft (75–100cm)	Any
C. rehderiana (syn. *C. nutans*)	Pale yellow tubular-shaped flowers with a cowslip scent. ¼–¾in (0·5–1·5cm) dia.	7 to 10	3	12¼–22¾ft (3·5–6·5m)	E, S, W
C. serratifolia	A native of Korea with sharply-toothed foliage and yellow lantern-like lemon-scented flowers 1½–2in (3–5cm) dia., followed by silky seed heads.	8 to 9	3	12¼–14ft (3·5–4m)	E, S, W
C. songarica	Non-climbing sub-shrub. Small yellowish-white flowers in clusters, scented.	6 to 10	3	5¼–7ft (1·5–2m)	E, S, W
C. stans	Herbaceous sub-shrub. Similar to *C. heracleifolia* but looser in habit. Flowers off-white, tubular ½in (1cm) dia.	9	3	3½–5¼ft (1–1·5m)	E, S, W
C. tangutica	Nodding yellow flowers 1–2in (2–5cm) dia. Attractive seed heads.	7 to 9	2 or 3	17½–24½ft (5–7m)	E, S, W
C. texensis '**Duchess of Albany**'	Pink bell-shaped flowers with red band 2–3in (5–8cm) dia.	7 to 10	3	8¾–14ft (2·5–4m)	E, S, W
C. texensis '**Etoile Rose**'	Deep cherry-pink bell-like flowers with silver-pink margins. 2–3in (5–8cm) dia.	7 to 9	3	8¾–14ft (2·5–3m)	E, S, W
C. texensis '**Gravetye Beauty**'	Ruby-red bell-shaped flowers that gradually expand to a star shape. 2–3in (5–8cm) dia.	7 to 10	3	8¾–14ft (2·5–4m)	E, S, W
C. texensis '**Sir Trevor Lawrence**'	Upright bell-shaped flowers of a luminous bright crimson-red shading to light violet at the edges. 2–3in (5–8cm) dia.	8 to 9	3	7–8¾ft (2–2·5m)	E, S, W
C. triternata '**Rubro-Marginata**'	Less vigorous than *flammula*. Small pink flowers with purplish edges. Scented.	8 to 10	3	17½–21ft (5–6m)	E, S, W
C. uncinata	Similar evergreen foliage to *C. armandii* but smaller leaves. Star-shaped white flowers in panicles. 1in (3cm) dia. Scented.	6 to 7	1	10½–15¾ft (3–4·5m)	Shelter or frost free
C. vedrariensis	Deep pink flowers of the *montana* type with yellow stamens. Scented, 2–3in (5–7cm) dia.	5 to 6	1	24½–35ft (7–10m)	Any

VARIETY	DESCRIPTION	FLOWERING MONTHS	PRUNING CODE	HEIGHT	PLANTING ASPECT
C. vedrariensis 'Highdown'	Pink flowers of the *montana* type complemented by downy bronze foliage. 2–3in (5–8cm) dia. flowers.	5 to 6	1	24½–35ft (7–10m)	Any
C. vitalba	The UK's native clematis ('Travellers Joy', 'Old Man's Beard'). Small greenish-white flowers followed by masses of silky seed heads. Flowers 1–2in (2–3cm) dia.	7 and 8	3	35–45½ft (10–13m)	Any
C. viticella	Small purple nodding flowers 1in (3cm) dia. A native of Southern Europe.	7 to 9	3	24½–35ft (7–10m)	E, S, W
C. viticella 'Alba Luxurians'	A white form of the above with green recurved tips. Dark stamens. 1–2in (3–5cm) dia.	7 to 9	3	17½–24½ft (5–7m)	E, S, W
C. viticella 'Etoile Violette'	Rich violet flowers with creamy stamens 2–3in (5–8cm) dia.	7 to 9	3	8¾–14ft (2·5–4m)	E, S, W
C. viticella 'Kermesina'	Deep crimson with red-brown stamens. 2–3in (3–5cm) dia. Flowers in profusion.	7 to 9	3	12¼–22¾ft (3·5–6·5m)	E, S, W
C. viticella 'Little Nell'	Creamy-white flowers with mauve edges, greenish stamens, 1–2in (3–5cm) dia.	7 to 9	3	12¼–14ft (3·5–4m)	E, S, W
C. viticella 'Mary Rose'	An old cultivar, similar to *vit.* 'Purpurea Plena Elegans'. Fully double but more spiky. A smoky amethyst colour.	7 to 9	3	10½–14ft (3–4m)	E, S, W
C. viticella 'Minuet'	Semi-nodding flowers. Sepals white with mauve veins and margins. 1–2in (3–5cm) dia.	7 to 8	3	10½–12¼ft (3–3·5m)	E, S, W
C. viticella 'Purpurea Plena Elegans'	An old double form of *viticella*; masses of rosette-shaped violet-purple flowers, 1–2in (3–5cm) dia.	7 to 9	3	12¼–22¾ft (3·5–6·6m)	E, S, W
C. viticella 'Madame Julia Correvon'	Wine-red with twisted sepals recurved at tips. 2–3in (5–8cm) dia.	7 to 9	3	7–10½ft (2–3m)	E, S, W
C. viticella 'Margot Koster'	Masses of rosy-red flowers up to 4in (10cm) dia.	7 to 9	3	7–8¾ft (2–2·5m)	E, S, W
C. viticella 'Royal Velours'	Very deep velvety purple sepals. The darkest colour of this group. 2–3in (5–8cm) dia.	7 to 9	3	12¼–22¾ft (3·5–6·5m)	E, S, W
C. viticella 'Venosa Violacea'	A large *viticella* flower, 2½–3in (6–8cm) dia. Sepals white with deep purple margins and veining.	6 to 8	3	10½–12¼ft (3–3·5m)	E, S, W

Index

Note Individual clematis names are only included if there are specific details about the type or there is an illustration of it. *See* pages 114–26 for a full list of varieties. Page numbers of illustrations are in *italic* type.